A HANDBOOK OF
TRADITIONAL LIVING II

STYLE & ASCESIS

RAIDO

A HANDBOOK OF TRADITIONAL LIVING

II

STYLE & ASCESIS

ARKTOS

LONDON 2020

Original title: *La Formazione del Militante della Tradizione Quaderno Numero Tre: 'L'uomo della Tradizone: Stile e Ascesi'*

ISBN	978-1-912975-73-0 (Paperback)
	978-1-912975-74-7 (Hardback)
	978-1-912975-75-4 (Ebook)
TRANSLATION	John Bruce Leonard
COVER & LAYOUT	Tor Westman

🌐 Arktos.com   🆕 fb.com/Arktos   🐦 @arktosmedia   📷 arktosmedia

CONTENTS

PART ONE
GENERAL ORIENTATIONS

PART TWO
VITA EST MILITARE

‘ Supposing we are able to interpret, not in its
  form — scholasticism is the tomb of doctrine — but in
  its spirit, the traditional doctrine transmitted to us by
  Guénon and Evola, we hold that we owe this ability:

1) to the Flame of which we are the custodians;
2) to the disindividualising effort that we attempt to
    preface to the Action we undertake;
3) to the organic deliberation of our Strategy.

Behind these points, which have their reflection in
the triad of *spirit, soul, body* ... the entire world of the
Tradition is summarised.

   This is the reason for which we hold that if one
loses sight of even one of these cardinal points, there
can be no serious revolt against the modern world.’

— GAETANO ALÌ

PREFACE

WHEN WE FIRST cut the pages of the booklet 'Working Unities'—this was in the year 1993—we were immediately impressed by the simplicity with which it laid out its project, aiming at the constitution of a solid organisation of traditional inspiration, composed of various groups, each with a specific scope for political and organisational action, and organically aiming at constituting, in the future, the Front of the Tradition. This project, proposed and realised by the community of militants of the *Centro Studi di Formazione Tradizionale 'Heliodromos'*,[1] is founded on a meta-historical principle: the Tradition. The document in which this was presented did not conceal the difficulty of its implementation, but nonetheless aroused in us enthusiasm and a proactive interest, oriented toward the constitution of a Working Unity.

In that period, the Roman territory was populated by a myriad of 'political' groups, whose goals were aimed exclusively at 'social' concerns, at the 'people', at national identity. In the past, we, too, adopted this attitude, puffed up with the slogan of 'revolution' and a nostalgic sentiment for the 'Italian nation'. By virtue of this experience, we can affirm that the attitude in question represented and represents now one of the many limitations set around the milieu of the Right. But there is another and yet graver illusion, which is at its root also a presumption: that of wishing to furnish solutions for the problems of

---

1   The Study Centre of Traditional Formation 'Heliodromos.' — Trans.

society without first occupying oneself with concretely realising a high model of reference which brings inner formation into the foreground. When the militant and organisational path proceeds (contrary to our own experiences) alongside an 'inner reconstitution', this translates into visible works — such as economic, cultural and political structures and activities of whatever kind you please — as the proof of a system of values which concretely reflects a system of life. Beyond this, the constitution of a territory is important, an uncontaminated island, a potential model of State, where it is possible to live according to rhythms long since forgotten by the man of the city. A true touchstone against the desert and the death brought by modernity.

Given the comatose state in which the Italian people languishes, and the waste of energy which might be required to convert it to a normal sense of life — as this would be equivalent to wishing to reanimate a sick person in the terminal stage — we have taken a step back, or probably two steps ahead, by coming to analyse and rectify our condition. We have reflected that it is absurd to propose projects when one does not yet possess the nature and the inner 'structure' to develop and govern oneself. We therefore decided to subscribe to the proposal of the Working Unities, to live through a formative experience different from that of the activist politics which we have always known. This path imposes on one the necessity of interiorising, day by day, the work undertaken, and to measure, at the same time, one's personal degree of responsibility toward the constitution of an authentic Organic Community. Leaving political activism, with its extempore posting of manifestos and flyers, behind us, we began to realise a new political action, aimed at recovering an ancient style founded on the values of Loyalty, Fidelity, Honour, Sacrifice and Hierarchy, crowned by the disposition toward Justice. Our objective became, and at present remains, that of creating paths which proceed above all toward revitalising in each person the predisposition toward Sacrifice and toward bearing witness to the Values by which we orient ourselves — apart, of course, from establishing economic and political structures which are

capable of financing themselves. This experience, which we hold to
be one of the few valid experiences today, we propose to all those, be
they groups or individuals, who have not yet 'found' their partipica-
tory identities and their path into the future; and we emphasise that
the project of Working Unities and the constitution of the Front of the
Tradition, which are inspired exclusively by the principles of Sacred
Order from which political action is born, is a necessary step for any
man who intends to redeem his dignity.

It is for this reason that our structures differ from 'modern' ones,
both quantitatively and qualitatively, since they move with ritual and
sacred rhythms, conscious of the fact that up until now nothing has
been done in the face of the strength of our enemies, and that we
would be called to do much more still.

We hold that this proposal is a major contribution.

ENZO IURATO

BORN AMONG THE RUINS

W HO TODAY ARE the men and women of the Tradition? In the face of the growing crisis of society, what comportment should they adopt? What is the ethic and existential model to which they ought to refer?

These are several questions that present themselves to whomsoever, having undertaken militancy for the Tradition, is sensitive to interior formation and finds himself standing before the many problems that daily life presents. For one such as this, it is not easy to undertake an action of testimony in a world lacking in every reference to the Sacred, a world in which every ethical norm has been neglected and betrayed. After having decreed the 'death of God', a new type of society has gained the upper hand in the course of the latest decades: it is a society without the least respect for human dignity, where the better part of human beings have been brutalised by profit and the abuses of power, by hypocrisy and cravenness. The system, be it in its liberal-capitalist form or in its socio-Marxist form, has reduced existence to a constant race to satisfy material needs, with the consequent atrophy of every superior perspective and the trampling of the foundations for all normal character and personality.

It is a simple thing to observe how the thousand daily worries that condition the individual leave him in a state of profound passivity, his mind 'elsewhere' — a state in which the greater part of his actions are performed lightly, as he is distracted and 'absent' to himself. One lives day by day; occurrences follow one another in a continuous and confused succession, actions and thoughts succeed each other obsessively, without any direction and orientation. One is vampirised by a mass of automisms that render one incapable of reacting to the degrading current. This is the condition of the greater part of modern men, who are forced to lead a superficial, flat, anonymous existence, in which it is easy to become the victim of one's own imagination, so that one believes oneself to be other than one is, and ends up no longer comprehending the true sense of life. In such a climate of atheism, misbelief and materialism, the 'elementary forces' — the maleficent throngs of *Gog and Magog*[1] — run amock, unleashing themselves without any control.

The State, religion, the family, school and any other institution which once attributed sense to the whole of human existence, have lost that central role in the formation of the individual, to such a degree that they are now mocked and derided, bereft of true respect and authority.[2] To what extent are men and women capable of living

---

1   In antiquity, *Gog and Magog* symbolically represented the savage and barbaric throngs, the carriers of destruction, pestilence and extermination. These populations, in numerous myths, take on the significance of formless masses, of obscure, chaotic and demonic forces that are halted in their forays by a 'wall', constantly monitored by sentinels in arms. When attention is withdrawn from this 'vigilance', disorder and injustice determine the *fissures or cracks in the Great Wall*. From these fissures Subversion worms its way in and assaults the organic order, to such a point that it overwhelms it completely. Cf. the important work of R. Guénon, *The Reign of Quantity and the Signs of the Times*.

2   The modern world, in all its aspects, presents a substantial sense of decadence and of emptiness, and whoever wishes to react to this subversive process is ever more alone: "'The desert grows. Woe to him who hides a desert in himself!" Indeed, he no longer finds outside of himself any support. The orders and institutions that in a traditional civilisation and society would have permitted him to realise himself integrally, to organise in a clear and unequivocal way his own existence, to defend and to apply, in his proper sphere and in a creative way, the

today, without the help of those supports proper to a normal society? In the face of such devastation, one must and one can react, but only by conforming one's existence to a law — a vision of the world: the Tradition — and adopting an iron discipline — a style of life: militancy (Formation).

For whomever feels himself to be a stranger in this world of decadence, for whomever does not wish to surrender to bourgeois hypocrisy, the first concern is to orient himself, to refer to a nucleus of Universal Principles that, by reason of their origin and transcendent nature, are eternal, atemporal, objective, immutable. To assume these Principles as 'normal' and 'spontaneous', living consistently in harmony with virtue — to *be* and not to *appear* to be— means to grasp the essence and the profound significance of Tradition.

Toward this end, the exhortation which Julius Evola presents in *Orientations* still has meaning: 'The first problem, the basis of every other, is that of inner character, of realising oneself, of being resurrected internally, of giving oneself form, of creating in oneself an order and a rule.'[3]

RAIDO

---

principal values he internally recognises, are today inexistent.' J. Evola, *Ride the Tiger*, Chapter 1.

3   J. Evola, 'Orientations', Point 2. The word I have translated here as 'resurrected' is *risorto*, which can also mean 'arisen' or 'arisen again', per the etymological origin of our own 'resurrect'. 'Rule' in the original is rather *una drittura*, literally 'a straightness', thus hearkening back also to the original sense of our 'rule', as line and *therefore* a law, a pattern. 'Orientations' can be read in full English translation in *A Handbook for Right-Wing Youth* (London: Arktos Media Ltd., 2017). — Trans.

PART ONE

General Orientations

1. THE PATH OF TRADITION

1.1 THE PRINCIPLES OF TRADITION

René Guénon in *The Crisis of the Modern World* affirms: 'if an idea is true, it belongs equally to all who are capable of understanding it; if it is false, there is no credit in having invented it. A true idea cannot be "new", for truth is not a product of the human mind; it exists independently of us, and all we have to do is to take cognizance of it; outside this knowledge there can be nothing but error.'[1] Julius Evola echoes him, stating the matter in the following way in his introduction to *Revolt Against the Modern World*: 'From our point of view there is nothing arbitrary, subjective or fantastical, and there is nothing objective or scientific, as the moderns understand these terms. None of this exists. All of this stands outside of the Tradition. The Tradition begins at that point where, by reaching a superindividual and non-human point of view, it is possible to place oneself above all of this. Thus one will have a minimal concern with discussing and "demonstrating". The truths that can make the world comprehend Tradition are not those that are "learned" or "discussed". They either are, or they are not.'[2]

---

1   R. Guénon, *The Crisis of the Modern World* (Hillsdale NY: Sophia Perennis, 2001), pp. 56–57.

2   J. Evola, *Revolt Against the Modern World*, 1969, Introduction.

For the man who follows the path of the traditional life, the Truth — 'that which is' — is given as something certain and absolute, and his task is to know it, aligning his life with it, given that beyond such Knowledge, lies error. Indeed, the Truth cannot be substituted and confused with a thought, an opinion, an ideology or a philosophical system; it is not a subjective interpretation or a human invention, since its reality and value, its essence and substance, are infallible, which is to say of Universal and Transcendent order, rather than being of a human or individual order. As with Truth, Justice, too, cannot be other than one and absolute; and beyond being correlated to and complimentary with one another (that which is true is also just and that which is just is also true), both are the realisation of the Universal Principle, from which all other Values and virtues derive.[3]

These are the Values that are points of reference and of verification, beyond being a valid support to orient one's entire existence: Honour, Loyalty, Fidelity, Sacrifice, Courage. This last is essential, because it allows one not to vacillate in that choice which, time after time, life calls one to perform and to confirm. Courage is the strength that permits one to dedicate oneself without setting conditions, to accept the hardest road in the face of a thousand obstacles, to take risks for that which one believes. To these, one should add Hierarchy, which etymologically means 'Sacred Order' (from the Greek ιερός, 'sacred', and αρχή, 'order, principle'); that is, the distinction of persons on the basis of the realisation of virtue, which is the incarnation of

---

3   It would be well to specify that, however many modes of expression and rapprochement one might find for defining or seeking the Truth, the essence of this latter cannot ever be disowned or counterfeited, nor restrained by mere relativism: Truth and Justice remain, always and in every case, unique, absolute and universal. At best, that man is limited and relative who undertakes the effort of knowing it and realising it, since he can deviate or deceive himself. The modern world, in this sense, with its errors and horrors (individualism, rationalism, equality, utilitarianism, relativism etc.) remains entrapped in deceit and lies insofar as, rejecting the absolute and the universal, it denies the possibility of knowing Truth and Justice.

the Principles. Hierarchy is an ascending stairway of quality and not quantity, real and not imaginary, which indicates one's belonging to a world wherein everyone is positioned in his right place, in accordance with a distinction and a qualitative differentiation of persons.

Altogether the Principles, one's connection to them, their being vitalised, their being the foundations and the basis for a civilisation, an institution and a rule of life, constitute the essence of the Tradition, outside of which lies the democratic world, the society of equality, of materialism and of individualism. The Values, let us repeat, are not negotiable; either they are absolute, universal and eternal, or else they are simple social and moral conventions, imposed by bourgeois and democratic relativism. And so, it is to be expected that the militant should form and inform his entire existence in accord with the Tradition, following the orientation of life indicated by the Principles and by virtue, forfeiting every whim, alibi or justification. Therefore, the attention turned toward the Sacred cannot be understood as a flight into the abstract, but rather as quest, struggle, affirming tension, fortitude, which represent the qualities of 'style' and 'heroic will'; and this stands in opposition to whatever issues from passivity or abandon. It is the attitude of whomever adopts for himself the motto, 'To bring oneself to that place from which one does not defend, but attacks'.

1.2 THE CHALLENGE OF THE TRADITION

The traditional doctrine affirms that the human being is, by his nature, an intermediate stage, a condition that must be overcome. Man finds himself in the centre, between the luminous angelic world of heaven and of the spirit on the one hand, and the dark region, the nether world of shadow and of chaos on the other. Between these two realities, there is an unspannable distance and an eternal battle, in which man participates in the space of his own earthly life, though it be brief, hurtling the challenge and making his choice. Indeed, it is not possible to remain indifferent here; one must choose between Truth and lie, Justice or oppression, Order or chaos, Light or shadow — between a vision of the world and of life oriented toward the Sacred and the heights, or an obscure existence, seduced by a thousand entice-ments, by the flatteries and the temptations of the modern world. Participation in one world rather than in the other is not the result of a theoretical or ideological elaboration, since belonging demands adhesion to a deeper and more intimate reality, which involves the whole of the human being. Belonging to the Front of Tradition creates impassible distances, characterised by the acceptance of obligations and responsibilities, which day after day remove the equivocations caused by one's own inconsistency.

According to Evola's definition, 'the Tradition is, in its essence, something metahistorical and, at the same time, something dynamic: it is a general ordering force, following principles which have the chrism of a higher legitimacy — if you please, it could also be said: of principles from the heights; it is a force which acts through the generations, in continuity with spirit and inspiration, through institu-tions, laws and orders that can also show a noteworthy variety and diversity.'[4]

To lead an upright life, rejecting vulgarity, injustice and duplicity, becomes the necessary foundation for re-establishing a connection with spiritual forces. One must be strong and determined, aware that every action one makes within the furrows of Tradition is a rite which nears man to heaven. In this respect, the practice of certain activities such as mountaineering, martial arts and parachuting can help to re-awaken in the individual the experience of a trial or the need to over-come, although it is important to clarify that these experiences must not be lived merely as sports or as an exaltation of the physical cult, nor in one's own individuality, but rather as a means of educating to discipline, of conferring to the person a form and a character. Beyond this, the militant must educate himself to reflection, to concentra-tion and that attention on himself, which is born from a doctrinal

---

4   Cf. J. Evola, *Men Among the Ruins*, Chapter 14, Section 2.

deepening — the aim of which is to reinforce his preparation, and to consolidate the truths toward which he might direct his action — and from the capacity to rediscover solitude and conversation with himself, distancing himself, as much as is necessary, from crowded and noisy places.[5] This attitude, ascetic and virile at the same time, clarifies the task that falls to the militant of the Tradition: life is a field of battle, a struggle to reappropriate one's own essence by realising, within oneself and around oneself, a harmonic order. This struggle is of a spiritual type, directed toward forming an Order, above all interior, and subsequently communal (together with men who lead the same battle on the same front), and later, finally, capable of manifesting, thanks to example, in the political, cultural, social and economic fields.

As an 'exile' one sets out on alien roads where life is soldiership,[6] where what is important is not to conserve, but to fight! To keep this clear means already to possess the capacity to create in oneself a system of defence against those snares and conditionings that originate outside of oneself. Toward this end, one should establish certain precise points of reference so as to reveal the elements of style: Justice, Truth, Beauty, Courage, Loyalty, Honour, Fidelity and Sacrifice should be taken as the foundations of daily life. One must put forth a dignity and a rectitude, which bear witness to an existence lived as authenticity, a style that is the tangible sign of a renewed inner tension which, repudiating every lie, knows how to awaken Love with knowledge and joy. And it is Evola who indicates to us the prime task which we must undertake, and who exhorts to it: 'And today what counts' — precisely and exclusively — 'is the work of whomever knows how to keep himself on the line of the mountain peaks: firm in his

---

5   Nietzsche affirmed: 'Loneliness can be the escape of the sick; loneliness can also be escape *from* the sick.' Cf. *Thus Spoke Zarathustra*, Part Three, 'Upon the Mount of Olives' (New York: The Modern Library, 1995).

6   Italian: *dove la vita è milizia*, lit. 'where life is militia'. Be it born in mind that both the Italian and our English come from the Latin *militia, -ae* meaning first of all 'work' or 'difficulty', and only subsequently 'soldiery' and also 'courage', hence also 'military spirit'. — Trans.

principles; inaccessible to any kind of concession; indifferent before fevers, before the convulsions of superstitions and the prostitutions to whose rhythm the last generations dance. All that matters is the silent keeping still of the few, whose impassible presence as "petrified guests"[7] serves to create new relations, new distances, new values.'[8]

In ordinary life, in every aspect of existence, a warrior's tension must be assumed, as in a struggle for the affirmation of Order against disorder. Only thus will the Tradition not be confused with an empty conformism, a sterile and useless moralism or a sentimental fact; only thus will the Tradition not be a simple 'evocation' or an empty rhetorical exercise, but the tangible witness of a profound and integral change in one's very essence.

1.3 TO FREE ONESELF FROM MASKS

One must look within oneself and recognise to what extent and in what circumstances one's very comportment is inconsistent with the principles by which one claims to live. On the one hand, one must analyse and vanquish one's weaknesses; on the other hand, one must fortify one's qualities and capacities, striking down the obstacles standing between fantasy and reality: between that which one claims to be and that which one really is. The fantasies and imaginings, the arrogance and presumption of believing oneself to be 'someone',

---

7   Italian: *convitati da pietra*, reference to the legend of Don Juan. The 1631 comedy of the Spaniard Tirso de Molina, entitled *The Deceiver of Seville and the Feast with the Stone*, was the first to introduce this idea, and the 1665 play of the French comic playwright Molière (1622–1673) was likewise entitled *Dom Juan or the Feast with the Stone*. The same Don Juan was the inspiration for Mozart's famous opera *Don Giovanni*. In the legend, Don Juan finds himself eating dinner with a statue of the man he has killed. The Italian phrase *convitato di pietra* thus comes to mean the oppressive presence of a person who is in fact absent. In the present case, by virtue of one's bearing and one's evident quality, one becomes by one's mere mute presence, a rebuke on those who live as the masses live. — Trans.

8   J. Evola, *Revolt Against the Modern World*, Introduction.

obstruct one from living and gaining awareness of what one really is, imprisoning one within a cage wrought of illusions, defeats and frustrations.

This first analysis, undertaken with the greatest sincerity, serves to liberate one from the many 'masks' that everyone wears every day, laying bare the small compromises with one's own cowardice and laziness, so as to favour a climate adapted to affirming Traditional Principles and virtues.[9] It is useless to act out the role of 'the hard and the pure' without being ready for an arduous labour of interior rectification, without being capable of imposing a discipline, of undertaking such labour with courage and simplicity, in which the sincere examination of conscience reveals one's limits and one's vices — conscious all the while of how painful all failure and all falling in style is, of the worthlessness of all short-cuts and guile. The Tradition, indeed, makes no concessions to human weaknesses, and whoever, in knowledge of books or in the grips of a revolutionary furore, does not follow a correct spiritual realisation, animated by an upright and consistent lifestyle, remains imprisoned on the level of pretty words and good intentions.

The task of the man of Tradition, therefore, begins with banishing every desire to be at the centre of attention, every whim; it begins, in other words, with being faithful to a discipline which is capable of forming character. This is the challenge: to recognise oneself and to define precisely one's place of belonging, creating distance and a border, as if it were a dam, between oneself and chaos. 'Men who are no longer recognisable for their badge or their card, but for their way of being ... . Indeed, to conquer oneself is more difficult than to conquer others; to combat an enemy who is mercurial and is master of the art of mimicry, lord of devious influences, ready to take advantage of every insufficiently firm moment, is more arduous than to triumph over

---

9   Masks are used in the theatre by actors who play as many characters. When one leaves the stage and continues to recite one's lines, one ends up believing that the mask is a true face, with the consequence of creating a 'double' personality, of falsifying oneself and reality.

an external and clearly distinguishable enemy, who is organised into subversive parties and in fractious action squads. For this it is necessary — as is said in military language — to "detach oneself", to create new distances, to posit new, tangible criteria of values, to liquidate the residues of democracy and of vacillation, through a closed elite which stands as an Order, and which is decisive, inexorable, over and above every subordinated power and every administrative dugout.'[10]

Belonging to one camp or another is no longer a question of ideological differences, which are artfully sustained by the modern world to bring false oppositions between Right and Left. The true difference is between the man who has a spiritual vision of life and of the world and the man who opposes himself to it in the name of a diabolic materialism.

The time has come to establish an interior distance from this society and from its modes of being; from all the needs, all the watchwords which aim to reduce the person to a product of the market; from every infatuation and deceptive illusion, by adopting to oneself the realistic style which knows how to look reality directly in the face, without hypocrisy or velleity. To be as ready sentinels, responsible and aware, means to affirm a style capable of distinguishing between the ideological allegiances at play.

'It is important, it is essential, that an elite be constituted, which, in a gathered intensity, with intellectual rigour and absolute intransigence, defines the idea by which its members will be united, and affirms this idea above all in the form of a new man, the man of resistance, the upright man amidst the ruins',[11] toward the end of 'silently preparing the right spiritual atmosphere, that the symbol of a super-elevated intangible authority should be felt and should acquire once more the fullness of its meaning.'[12]

---

10   J. Evola, *Carattere* (Catania: Edizione Il Cinabro, 2005), pp. 63–64.

11   J. Evola, 'Orientations', Point 11.

12   Ibid., Point 7.

2. THE DIFFERENTIATED MAN

2.1 PRESENT-DAY ACTIVISM

OUTSIDE OF THE traditional Law, action is a passive and confused fretfulness, because it is devoid of any meaning and any higher orientation. In the contemporary, materialistic and desacralised society, the existence of man is a continual movement, a succession of gestures performed often unconsciously, a 'doing' which is transformed into a true agitation in every direction. It is not consciousness which leads the way here, so much as the lack of any points of reference.

Activism, whose characteristic is 'to act for action's sake' — that is to say for the glorification of the irrational, the triumph of the vitalistic leap, the exaltation of a fever of becoming — makes of man an unconscious sleepwalker. "I am absorbed by my thoughts, by my memories, by my desires, by my suggestions, by the steak that I eat, by the cigarette that I smoke, by the love that I make, by the nice weather, by the rain, by this tree, by this motorcar that passes, by this book." Thus we are the shadows of ourselves."[1]

The days, the weeks, the months run by us each the same as the last, chasing after something, whose meaning we at bottom do not understand, stressed as we are by the frenzied pace imposed by society. The same society which on the one hand teaches us to run a thousand

---

1   J. Evola, *Ride the Tiger*, Chapter 10.

miles per hour to affirm our ego in careers, in wealth and success, in pleasure and in unlimited well-being, and on the other hand proposes entertainment and distraction as an alternative. And so arises the desire to dull one's senses, to think of nothing, to let oneself go, to release the tension and to forget oneself,[2] to grow heady on life or to make life grow heady on oneself, in a sort of anti-depressive euphoria. In both cases, we are witness to the exaltation of the vital force, the search for different and ever stronger emotions, the necessity of redefining oneself continually through new and original forms. We look upon two faces of the same medallion, in which man lives outside of himself, in a state of apparent awareness, but incapable of controlling or directing a life which is the succession of habits and conditionings: a cog within a larger machine. For even when he 'stops' himself, or better to say, interrupts his racing about, in reality he continues his frenetic pacing in a different form, increasingly resembling a hamster running on its wheel within its cage. Life reaches the limits of 'nonsense', an existence deprived of certainties and prospects, in which one adopts the philosophy of 'seize the moment', the *carpe diem* that knows no future.

Given this state of things, the first step is to become aware of one's situation. The crisis of present-day society, even before it assaults institutions and the political apparatus, is a distortion of the human being in his integrity. Therefore, to reconquer a character and a style of action is the single true alternative to the existential condition of whomever lives alienated by a thousand preoccupations, and at the same time entrapped in the veritable escape routes which have been laid out to impede and neutralise any possible interior reaction.

---

2   Italian: *uscire da sé*, literally 'to exit oneself'. — Trans.

2.2 DIFFERENTIATED ACTION

Contemporary society presents itself ... as an organism which has passed from the human type to the subhuman, in which every activity and every reaction is determined by the needs and by the tendencies of pure physical life. Its dominant principles are exactly those proper to the physical part.[3]

The rectification of the militant requires him to pass through his present instinctive and subhuman 'animal' plane to the human plane, reconquering the dignity and the identity which the modern world has buried. Though he lives in this world, the militant feels himself internally to be alien to it; he does not belong to it and does not wish to belong to it, refusing every compromise with it.[4]

He does not behave as a delinquent or a degenerate, but assumes the style and the spirit of the warrior, and, though he must live with a thousand difficulties, he does so with honour and dignity. He is neither desperate nor inept, actuated or agitated by his dissatisfactions; he is far from following the model of the social climber or the social justice warrior. He is different from other men because he has fixed, at the centre of his own being, the force of the Tradition — the Sacred; he is conscious that the reality in which he lives has nothing any longer of the natural and the spiritual about it. He is a 'rebel' with a path to follow, an exacting and, at the same time, fatiguing destination to attain: the reconquest of himself. For him the ancient teaching holds true: 'to know oneself in order to be oneself'. He does not accept compromises and is not a reformist, one who wishes to change or to improve the

---

3   J. Evola, *Revolt Against the Modern World*, Chapter 35, 'The Regression of the Castes'.

4   The militant understands those who, like him, align themselves against this world, be they even the 'maladjusted' or the 'asocial', but he remains distant and detached from the misadventures of such men, without justifying or accepting them. Indeed, he is not a conscious objector, an outcast or an anarchist, because he is not prisoner to their hatred, which aims to destroy without offering any valid alternatives.

social and political order. His alternative to the system is a complete alternative; he seeks no reform of it, but rather he hopes for its total overcoming. He is not an abstract type who lives of imagination, but he is the carrier of a concrete project of renovation.

His choice is free, conscious and responsible. He commits himself to reawakening a new and more intransigent realism. 'The "style" that must come to the fore is the style of the man who holds his position in faith with himself and with an idea, in a gathered intensity, in the rejection of every compromise, in a total commitment that must manifest itself not only in the political struggle, but also in every expression of existence: in the factories, in the laboratories, in the universities, in the streets, in one's own personal and emotional life.'[5] The important thing for him is that he does not perform unworthy acts, acts for which he might feel ashamed; he adopts as his own the law of honour which demands that he never be vile, not even with his bitterest enemy. He despises every contemptible act, such as deceit, theft, slander, pusillanimity; he holds in the highest esteem every attitude of loyalty, sincerity, honour, consistency. He is fortified by love of discipline and hierarchy; he desires clear and loyal relations, manly relations; he has a disposition to Courage, an innate sense of Honour and Fidelity, capable of developing themselves to the point of sacrifice.

His is an ethic of responsibility; he affirms a sense of duty free of rhetoric, a heroism without glory, without triumphs, medals or great deeds, without the mania for originality or fame. He is characterised by an internal style, the capacity of keeping oneself lucid and present to oneself, a calm and a transparency that reveal equilibrium and harmony, which aim at interior fortitude, at the consistency of intentions, at the adoption of duties and responsibilities. It is the style of whomever chooses the hardest road; it is the legionary spirit of whomever, by his destiny, loyally undertakes that which costs the most, and does not avoid the hard and even the risky life.

---

5   J. Evola, 'Orientations', Point 3.

To live an existence permeated by spiritual Values means to take a different approach to reality, to affirm a style deriving from the effort of overcoming the vile and bourgeois human nature, by means of an inexorable and radical change. The militant has a different way and quality of seeing things; different is his attention to every action he performs, for he is constantly measuring himself against his responsibilities. In this way action translates into 'form*ation*', that is, bringing an order within one's life, and in 'rectific*ation*',[6] that is, discipline and ascesis, conforming oneself to the Tradition, to a spiritual rule which governs one's existence. A law which unites the person with his community, with his people, with his bloodline,[7] in a belonging and a cultural identity.

Rectification and formation are the watchwords, continually tending toward a reconnection with a force which originates from the heights, through an action which is 'cathartic' and 'anagogic'. We are dealing with 'a mastered attitude, an enlightened audacity, a concise and convinced word, a decision which is as precise and consistent as it it is deliberate, a cold sense of dominion, without personalism and without vanity ..., clear-cut action without grand gestures, realism which does not at all mean materialism, but rather love for the essential; the ideal of clarity ...; diffidence in the face of every kind of abandon of the soul and for every confused mysticism; intolerance for every tortuous dialectic; a natural predominance of *ethos* over *pathos*;

---

6   The play on words is etymologically valid in English, but not quite as clear as in Italian: 'form*azione*' and 'rettific*azione*' where *azione* means *action*. *Formation* would thus be the forming of action; rectification, the *rectifying* of action; and given the origin of rectify from the Latin *rectus*, 'straight' (which etymology is much more evident in Italian, on account of its pure Romance heritage), this in turn means, making one's action straight, bringing order into one's action. — Trans.

7   The Italian is *stirpe*, which can also mean *race* (distinguished from the more historically charged word *razza*) or *stock*. The idea encapsulates the *ethnic heritage* of a person. — Trans.

a love for limit; the capacity to coordinate oneself in view of an idea and of a higher order.'[8]

2.3 ACTION BECOMES RITE

As Julius Evola reminds us: 'Already in common life a discipline should be followed, apt to make one aware of the uselessness of every sentimentalism and of every affective complication. In the place of these things, the lucid glance and the fit act.[9] As with the surgeon: in the place of compassion and pity, the cut which resolves the problem. As with the warrior and with the sportsman: in the place of fear, of irrational agitation in the face of danger, the ready determination for all that which is given one to do. Pity, fear, hope, impatience, anxiety are all fracturings of the soul, which come sooner or later to nourish occult and vampiric powers of negation. Take compassion: it removes nothing of the evil which afflicts another, but causes that evil to disturb your soul. If you can, act, adopt the person of the other and communicate your strength to him. If you cannot, detach yourself. Thus too for hatred: it is degrading to hate. If you wish, if the justice in you wishes it,[10] overthrow, cut down, without upsetting your soul.'[11]

The action of the militant is thus quite different than activism, insofar as it is undertaken with detachment from the passions and from the desires, from the yearning of the senses and of the imagination, through the will and the discipline of him who wishes to reaffirm his

---

8   J. Evola, *Carattere*, op. cit., pp. 22–23.

9   Italian: *l'atto adeguato*, meaning the act that is proper, that is suitable, that is fitting with respect to what must be done. — Trans.

10   Italian: *se giustizia vuole in te*, literally 'if justice wants in you'. The central element appears to be that impersonal and impartial justice acts *through* one, that one becomes the vehicle of justice rather than the agent of justice. — Trans.

11   J. Evola, *Introduction to Magic as a Science of the Ego*, Vol. 1, 'On the Magical View of Life'.

self-control.[12] It is the free and impersonal action which is the fruit of sacrifice, capable of transforming action itself into rite.

He concerns himself with undertaking that which must be done, without troubling himself over the fruits of his work, with firm impartiality and without complaining about the 'might be' or 'if only'. 'One must know how to renounce anything the moment one feels that it has become necessary to one, the moment one discerns desire or pleasure in it; in principle one must do, not what one wants, but whatever costs one something; in principle one must always take the path of greatest resistance and, with this, must render one's will ever strong and purer, one's self-possession ever more energetic.'[13]

This action is control of irrational movement, of the instincts or the perturbations of the soul, capable of gradually breaking through the 'crust' of habits and vices that prohibit the re-emergence of the true nature of men. Greatness of character does not consist in being bereft of sentiments or passions, but in knowing them and possessing them to the greatest degree and, as if they were 'sirens' seeking to divert one from one's duty, to refrain from obeying them, in a dominion which is the expression of one's will. It will be as though one crosses a destructive place without being destroyed; it is not at all inappropriate, then to define oneself a warrior, since the warrior is that type of man who recognises in the aptitude to courage, in the mastery of oneself, in the capacity to sacrifice oneself without regard for gain, the way to one's realisation.

In *Revolt Against the Modern World*, Julius Evola affirms: 'Free are they who, taking this traditional direction, do not feel it as an

---

12 This vision is to act without acting. In the Tao Té Ching, the following is affirmed: 'To create without possessing / To act without appropriating / To lift oneself without effort / This is the way' (19), and again: 'The way of Heaven is: / Not to fight and still to win / To make oneself obeyed without commanding / To attract without calling / Calm, this brings everything to fulfilment' (73). Cf. *The Tao Té Ching* (edited by J. Evola), E.M. 1997.

13 J. Evola, *I saggi di Bilychnis* ('The Essays of Bilychnis'. Padova, Edizioni Ar: 1987), p. 30.

imposition, but develop themselves spontaneously, they recognise themselves in it, to such an extent that they are capable of actuating, almost as though in a movement from within, the highest "traditional" possibility of their nature. The others, those who materially and obediently follow institutions, but without understanding them and living them, are sustained by these institutions: however much they might be bereft of light, their obedience carries them virtually beyond their limitation as individuals, and sets them upon the same direction as the others. But for those who follow neither in spirit nor in form the traditional course, there is naught but chaos. They are the lost, the fallen."[14]

Free, therefore, is the militant who learns to know and to control himself, after a serious and hard labour of ascesis, in which the Values are lived and not preached. The classical world, in this regard, knew how to distinguish the liberty *to do* something, which can go so far as arbitrariness, from the liberty *for doing* something, which is the power of actuating one's own qualification, through the observance of a law and a discipline. The second type of liberty is true liberty, which differentiates men in accord with justice. He who obscures his own conscience, on the other hand, abandoning himself passively to the instincts, cannot be called free.

2.4 THE HOLY WAR

Rectification is not in and of itself a mental process, but an operation which involves the whole being of man, a rediscovery of one's deepest essence. To the extent to which thoughts and actions are not effectively oriented by (and toward) the Tradition, one remains in the field of dialectic, academic and pseudo-intellectual exercise, which has nothing in common with formation and rectification.

In every traditional teaching, the work of rectification is called 'Holy War', to be fought so as to reappropriate one's own being to

---

14   J. Evola, *Revolt Against the Modern World*, Chapter 20, 'Man and Woman'.

oneself, realising within oneself the Sacred Order. The 'Holy War' is divided into the 'Lesser Holy War', represented by the battle against exterior enemies, and the 'Greater Holy War', evocative of a disindividualised action that goes beyond action itself and becomes a battle against the enemies that man bears within himself. The various trials of life are occasions to know oneself and to verify one's qualification; existence is a field of battle on which to measure oneself. It is a battle against enemies that nestle within the folds of the soul; it is a battle, of a spiritual and interior order, of the transcendent element (Spirit) against whatever is tied to desire, to natural instinct and to uncontrolled passion, one's lower nature. Victory can come only if one possesses an inner orientation, if at one's centre is placed an immobile point which, supposing it be identified and conquered, will permit rectification from every conditioning.

The man of Tradition can be recognised by the predominance of *ethos* over *pathos* in him, an ascesis and an interior simplicity which translates into the control and the management of impulses, emotions and sensations. A superiority that is calm and detached, not indifferent; a true superiority which is translated into 'style', dignity, self-possession, composure and lucidity. Being central to oneself means reconnecting oneself to a force which originates from the heights, the 'non-human force' of the transcendent Principle, capable of dominating, recomposing and organising every element of the lower nature, which is to say, every purely human element.

Toward this end, to commit oneself constantly over time is an optimal exercise to measure one's will, insofar as it is more difficult than seizing on the impetus or the force generated by an impromptu action. Weariness, the apparent uselessness of the work undertaken, or solitude can indeed act and corrupt the will in a much more devious way than an imminent battle or an immediate physical risk; but tenacity is a characteristic proper to the way of action. Moreover, one must also, insofar as it is possible, lead an essentialist life, simple and austere, where moderation in eating, in sleeping, in drinking and in diversions becomes an incentive, a sign of one's readiness and to never lower one's guard.

Some might be frightened by the weight of the commitment that they must bear, by the doubts that assault them, by the laziness or the lowliness that will surface in them despite their best intentions. There are deep voices which make themselves heard, especially in the most difficult moments of life, when fatigue or discouragement lay bare one's weaknesses.[15] There are critical phases which pose certain question to the militant, and his response must originate from an inner strength capable of reawakening, and from the capacity to pass over to counter-attack with firmness and decision, without abdicating his will and dignity. "'Unhappy is the man who has never confronted misfortunes and suffering', writes Seneca, 'because he has never had occasion to put his capacities to the test and to know them. To man has been conceded something better than mere exemption from evils: the power to triumph within himself. And those beings who have been tried most severely must be considered as the most valorous, if we bear in mind that in war the commanders entrust the most embattled positions to the strongest and best qualified men, while to the weakest and the least trustworthy are reserved the less difficult, but also the less glorious, positions of the rearguard.'"[16]

Even if at the beginning, things are hardest, when habits and vices re-emerge and enforce themselves with ever greater insistence, the man who aspires to a higher conception of life and liberty must joyfully follow the path of self-knowledge. The deepest happiness is found in the command of oneself, and only then can true liberty arise — the positive attitude and sovereign affirmation that, as I am, so I wish to be.

---

15   Cf. C. Z. Codreanu, *Il Capo di Cuib*, edizioni Ar and F. Bradescu, *Le tre prove legionarie*, Edizione Novantico.

16   J. Evola, *Oriente e Occidente* (Rome. Edizione Mediterranee: 2001), pp. 61 and 62. Equally significant is Seneca's pronouncement in *De Providentia* (IV, 3), which concludes: 'I say that you are unhappy, because you have never been unhappy.'

3. THE TWO RACES: ARISTOCRACY AND DEMOCRACY

3.1 DEMOCRACY AND THE CORRUPTION OF MAN

THE PALTRY MORALITY which marks humanity is the reflection of the disintegration proper to the democratic system: corrupt, individualist, materialist and desacralised. A climate of deviancy and social disorder 'brings up' fickle individuals, devoid of identity and any means of inner defence, incapable of distinguishing the true from the false, the just from the unjust, the normal from the abnormal. The inversion of Values has become so common that honesty, goodness and nobility of soul are ridiculed: the absurd predominates overall.

This situation is the consequence of a clear and carefully studied strategy for keeping the individual insecure, agitated and intent on racing after a thousand problems and needs — thus producing men who are incapable of thinking with their own heads, who are deprived of the capacity for analysis and introspection and who, once they have been emptied and sifted out, are like perfect poultry. By way of example, let it suffice for us to consider how man today is exposed to the assault of consumerism, one of the many instruments with which

Subversion has unhinged the ancient Traditional structures. Through the media, one is continually bombarded by messages whose aim is the creation of new and ever more useless and superfluous needs; the more objects are advertised, the more they become indispensable, with a consequent growth in the desire to purchase and possess them.[17] The possibility of being able to acquire everything one desires, perhaps through some manner of 'payment plan', creates the illusion of freedom in modern man, while in reality there are others who think and decide for him, who tell him how to live, what to eat, how to think and above all what to buy. Today, 'what one is' no longer counts, nor does the dignity, identity and the value of a person, but only 'what one has', which is to say, a tidy sum in the bank, a new car, a nice house, fashionableness, the latest Smartphone or tablet — thus causing a frenetic anxiety to appear eternally happy and successful. It is the great triumph of having over being.[18] It is therefore important to not further confuse things by thinking, as the Marxist positivists and the liberals do, that the overcoming of so much degeneration might come only through an improvement and a modification of the system. The

---

17   Let us consider commercials: a constant optimism oozing hypocrisy and falsity, the exaltation of a virtual society (in which everyone loves everyone, because they are all united by the latest Smartphone), where there is a complete sharing of nothing, where everyone knows everyone but no one knows who anyone truly is, where the superficiality of human relations and of existential experiences generates a life at once stressful and insipid.

18   The paradox is that this occurs at a historical period of great crises or economic disturbances, whose effect — which is, to put it mildly, comical and schizophrenic — is families that are unable to get to the end of the month, because they do not have a stable job or income, but who, at the same time, are incapable of renouncing that accessory item which would make the difference — that object which causes people to consider a man respectable. The institutions, on whatever level they stand, repeat the lullaby of sacrifices, of the tears and blood necessary to set the economy running once again, with its countless taxes and tithes to pay. But at the same time, in this society of images, where everything is media and communications, the message for human progress is always the same: consume/produce/die even if you have no money; consume/produce/die even if you have no house and cannot put food on your table.

problem, in point of fact, lies not with the so-called superstructures, which obviously contribute in a determinant way; the problem lies rather with the inner and personal nature: whatever rebirth is possible will derive first of all from an ethical and moral regeneration of the individual man. In this regard, C. Z. Codreanu, the Captain of the Iron Guard, used to say, 'Wars are won by those who knew how to attract the mysterious forces of the invisible world from the skies and to assure the collusion of these forces. ... In the last analysis, victories do not depend on material preparation, on the material strength of the combatants, but on their capacity to secure control over spiritual powers.'[19] To enunciate formulae and programmes, to convene organisational meetings, to create new movements or political parties, is secondary and absolutely contingent work; it follows upon the formation of the militant. 'We have no need of new programmes, but rather of new men', as C. Z. Codreanu put it; or again, as Julius Evola clarifies, the militant knows that 'the measure of what can still be salvaged depends on the existence, or the lack thereof, of men who stand forth, not to promulgate formulae, but to be examples — not by coming to terms with demagoguery or the materialism of the masses, but by reawakening other forms of sensation and interest.'

Everyone is, therefore, the artificer of his own destiny, and it is his way of being which informs the world surrounding him. 'Here is a principle which today more than ever ought to have absolute saliency: if a State were to possess a political or social system which, in theory, could be considered as the most perfect, but the human substance were crippled, this state would sooner or later descend to the level of the lowest society; while a people, a race capable of producing true men, men of just feeling and sure instinct, would reach a high level of civilisation and would keep its feet before the most calamitous trials, even were its political system lacking and flawed.'

---

19   C. Z. Codreanu, *Il Capo di Cuib*, op. cit., p. 49.

Indeed, man is poised between two worlds: one constituted by the noble, virtuous, true, beauty-loving, loyal, faithful and honest man who is master of himself (the Roman-aristocratic element); the other constituted by the vulgar, arrogant and vile, mediocre man, incapable of any aspiration which is not dictated by the most wretched egoism (the Mediterranean-democratic element). Between these two human typologies there exists a neat distinction, being as they are the limits of two opposite races: the first is oriented toward the heights, toward being and divinity, and his nature seeks and wants Order and virtue, so that he adopts to himself a law and a discipline, masters his own human nature and rules it in a higher dimension; the second, the dark nature, is oriented toward the lowly and toward becoming, toward the whole of material and contingent nature, where the human element and the senses (the generators of the material image of the world) are exalted. This distinction is neither political nor social; it has nothing about it of the abstract or the ideological, but it is deeper and more intimate because it defines two camps, two ways of being, two opposite visions of the world: on one side the metaphysical and luminous reality, on the other the nether and telluric nature.[20]

3.2 THE TRAUMATISED MAN AND THE MAN OF ELUSIVE RACE

The typology of modern man, who has been domesticated and rendered slavish, was defined by Julius Evola as 'the evasive race': 'Indeed, it might be argued that the 'democratic' climate is, in the long run, bound to exert a regressive influence on the very personality of man, even in 'existential' terms — precisely by virtue of the aforementioned correspondences between the individual as a small organism and the State as a large organism. ... But what has been extolled as the 'liberation' of this or that people and its 'democratic progress' ... is matched

---

20 It would be an error to speak of two counterpoised metaphysical realities here, both because Metaphysics, being Universal and One,

today in a significant number of individuals by a 'liberation' amounting to the elimination of any inner 'form', any sort of character, any kind of rectitude. What we find, in other words, is the decline or absence in the individual of that central power which I have already referred to with the evocative Classical denomination of *hegemonikon*.'

Suffice it to glance about oneself to realise the ever-greater number of formless and evasive people; people who are, to put it in a word, 'oblique'. These are individuals who favour exhibitionism, vanity, believing themselves to be important and, as often happens in politics, individuals who are arrogant and presumptuous, careless of the role which they ought to perform and of the service they ought to render.[21]

Oblique man is indeed devoid of humility and holds himself to be infallible; he comports himself in a conceited fashion; he is inclined to anger, to violence, to hatred and to slander; he is by nature envious and sectarian, and reduces human relations to simple opportunistic calculus. Ignoring every principle of solidarity, he acts exclusively for his own advantage. He seems to be the bearer of a genuine 'inferiority complex', which often translates into megalomania, with the consequence that he believes himself to be in continual competition with everyone and everything. Cowardly and false, he adopts the 'herd morality', sacrificing his own conscience so as to be liked by others — but he would not hesitate, if he could, to crush them and stand over them. His morality is empty conformism and hypocritical convention, his objective is personal gratification; he thinks and lives only for the pursuit of his own gain and his own egoistic pleasure. By nature he is maliciously curious and gossipy; he promises something but does not keep his promise; he forgets his commitments and is never punctual; he is a distracted and inconstant type, he knows no sense of distance, respect, discretion, chastity, hierarchy and authority. Sometimes he

---

21 Even in the 'milieu of the Right' itself, one happens to encounter 'personages' who, in the grips of a genuine ambition to command and to have a following, feel the need to build up a group of followers at every cost, without, in most of these cases, having the least capacity or qualification to lead it.

seems even 'brilliant', but his intuition is guided not so much by true intelligence, as by ability and slyness, since for him what is important is not being just, but knowing how to 'make fools' out of others, and, in the meantime, being exceedingly capable of dodging obstacles and circumventing laws through a thousand pretexts and expedients. He easily abandons himself to vulgar and uncouth attitudes, both in his expression and in his emotion — as is characteristic of a chaotic and disorderly life. Being unsure of himself, he easily becomes nervous, raising his voice out of mere caprice. His superficiality is observed in many inconclusive behaviours which flow into insignificant bullying, noisy and undisciplined exuberance, neurotic gesticulations. He possesses an undeniably bad taste. Only with difficulty is he able to concentrate and to be by himself; he must always 'dull his senses' and to keep to crowded places. He lives day by day, incapable of giving himself over to a discipline and to an interior form. He is inclined to commotion and to suggestion; he often exalts himself one moment and tears himself down the next. On the other hand, character and discipline are impossible for this kind of human being; he neither wants them nor possesses them. As a man he is altogether passion, pleasure, rhetoric, instinct; he is as romantic and sentimental as he is violent and obfuscating.

This is the complete portrait of the 'extreme' characteristics which, in part or in whole, can be found in contemporary man. With enough honesty, it is easy to perceive how they live also within us. At bottom, the challenge of the warrior resides precisely here: conscious of our limitations, we must dedicate ourselves to rectifying our character, through the formation and the affirmation of the style proper to the New Man.

3.3 TRADITIONAL ORIENTATION: THE VIRTUE OF THE NOBLE MAN

Opposed to the 'evasive' man is the New Man, the noble man, the warrior who finds his rootedness in the Principles that made the Roman Civilisation great. He posits as the centre of the whole of existence the respect for Truth and Justice and, in comparison with the sly man who concerns himself with his own gain or his own gratification, his entire life is oriented and ordered on the affirmation of the Values, as a corollary to virtue.[22] Within the democratic system, where every man claims for himself a presumed liberty and vested rights, it is demanding and complicated to realise such a task. On the other hand, in Traditional civilisation, the inclinations or the propensities of a vitiated nature were corrected or yoked by the climate of the general structure and of the institutions; these functioned thanks to (spiritual) sustainment from the heights which monitored the corrupt comportment of man. Nonetheless, given that we are called to work in the present epoch, the aspirations of those who do not recognise themselves in this world must be followed by the will to discipline, capable of restoring a form, a style and a way of being.

As the basis for the inner reconstruction of the New Man, it is useful to indicate a few characteristics proper to the Roman Man, the *Vir* — characteristics which we report in abbreviated form, but which we have already addressed in the previous sections.

Pietas, purity of heart, respect for the Sacred Reality sensed as present and active in the world. It is an inner penetration of the deep

---

22 In Latin, the term *virtus* (Virtue) has the same roots as *vir*, the noble man (as in virility), which is distinct from simple *homo*, the common man, put into relation with *humus*, earth. In Greek, Virtue is translated by ἀρετή (areté), whose root αρ- (ar) brings us back to the irregular superlative of the adjective, ἀγαθός (good), ἄριστος (aristos), that is, the best, from which derives the political form of *aristocracy*, the government of the best or of the fittest to govern, where the best are those who comport themselves in a virtuous way, so that political governance is rightfully theirs.

sense of the truth and the justice, of the harmony and the order which rules the Universe. It is duty before Divinity, before our ancestors, our parents, before the elderly and the weakest, before our bloodline, without falling into a sentimentalism which is as stupid as it is sterile. It is an affirmative attitude before the Divine, making certain that every action, thought or word is aimed at the realisation of the true, of the just and of the beautiful, in a transfiguration such as to render action into a rite, which is to say a real vivification of the Sacred. It is a permeation of traditional symbols even in those expressions which are apparently the least significant, eliminating all superficiality and disorder, living in harmony with the cosmic rhythm and leading a healthy, balanced and natural life. It is divine love perceived as real and present, as the fountainhead of joy and serenity.

Fidelity and **Loyalty**, the foundation of all justice, which would give 'each what is his own'. Evola, in this regard, explains: 'And something essential will be attained when love for a style of active impersonality is once again awakened, in which what counts is the work and not the individual, so that one is capable of considering oneself to be unimportant, since what is important is rather the function, the responsibility, the task assumed, the end pursued.'[23] It is the rejection of all egalitarian levelling, the discovery in hierarchy of a value to make one's own. It is the respect for one's given word, even when keeping it brings adverse and unexpected situations, since the faithful and loyal man, who does not think only of himself, his own advantage and his own image, acts impersonally, in a continual spirit of service in giving and in giving himself, without posturing (sacrifice). This is not the fidelity of a servile being, but of him who, following a free and conscious choice, adopts a responsibility with seriousness and awareness.

Dignity or **Honour**, commensurate with calmness and an inner dominion (serenity and poise), with living in honesty and decorum, even in small daily actions. The New Man is not moved by pettiness

---

23   J. Evola, *Orientations*, Point 4.

and cowardice; he is responsible and he rejects indolence and caprice. Nor is he venal or neglectful; nor does he live in a parasitic way.

Discipline, the will and the love for a stern self-control and mastery of oneself; diffidence for every abandonment of soul and control over all agitated actions. This is a just moderation, knowing how to give rule and right conduct to the body; it is a lucid self-presence, having the capacity to live without being overwhelmed by emotions or fears. Discipline is not limitation, but an attempt to react to chaos, instability and the contemporary restlessness. Acting in conformity with the rules of the traditional doctrine, one acquires character, which is indispensable for the affirmation of a true freedom from need.

Courage, virile firmness, the strength of soul that manifests as tenacity and perseverance in both success and failure, in the face of any adversity and suffering. An audacity devoid of rashness, which knows its own limits and its own strengths and is capable of transforming itself into clear action. The man gifted with courage, though he be conscious that his path presents obstacles of every kind, pains, displeasures and fears, does not retreat; no, but he takes heart and advances as a victor. This is a courage which is to be turned in the first place against one's defects, against the mental inertia which limits one and makes one passive. For the courageous man, living does not mean preserving oneself, but rather battling against the forces of chaos to re-establish order and light.

Simplicity, that is, adopting a sober, stern, precise and conscious style, through a love for the essential, realism and clarity. The militant lives life in a continual confrontation with himself and with the reality which surrounds him. His objective is above all to better himself. Conscious of his limits, he faces trials with the certainty of fighting for a just and holy cause. His only question is whether that which he performs respects truth and justice; if so, then he acts without indecision, in an energetic and detached way. He forces himself to be the best he can be and to better himself, constantly analysing himself and his actions.

Chastity, decency and reserve, united into a purity of heart. The militant must commit to eliminating haughtiness and insolence, vanity and arrogance, useless rhetoric in speaking and in working. His realism and his moderation are the manifestations of the serenity and the inner peace which dominate irrational and disorderly reaction. This is love of distance devoid of ambition and gratification; it is not letting oneself be carried away by wrath. The chaste man rejects the vulgarity and the brutalisation of the human being, in all its forms.

Wisdom, which is to say wise reflection, the capacity for attention and concentration, compassion for the errors and the limitations of others, and an equal intransigence toward one's own. It is wisdom matured by a doctrinal knowledge commensurate with one's experience of life; it is prudence combined with the incisiveness of that man who knows his own capacities and his own limits. The wise man is not an illusionist who violates reality when it suits him, deceiving himself or others with his desiderata; he is a man who observes and knows things for what they are, and not for what he would like them to be. His actions are balanced and sure and, whenever he must act, he evaluates the correct way to undertake a task so as to bring it to term in the best way possible.

4. THE PATH OF GREATEST RESISTANCE

4.1 INDIVIDUALISM AND VITALISM

ACCORDING TO THE Traditional vision, man is considered a person, a respectful participant in a communitarian organisation — be it the family, the people, the State — a bearer of rights, but principally of duties, gifted with an identitarian kind of belonging. In modern society, on the contrary, man is an *individual*, whose traits are substantially opposed to those of the person, to the point that his characteristic individualism and egocentrism permit the affirmation of the morality of 'minding one's own business', independently of any kind of belonging and solidarity of the communitarian kind: the social disorder which derives therefrom is inevitable and almost a given.

The individual, by definition, is an abstraction, numbered and formless entity, an atom unto itself, which possesses in itself no quality. And the individualism from which it derives is defined by Guénon as 'the negation of every principle superior to the individuality' and at the same time as 'the general reduction of civilisation to simply human elements'.[1] Many of the characteristics at the bottom of the modern

---

1   Cf. R. Guénon, *Precisazioni necessarie* (Padova: Edizioni Ar, 1988), *The Reign of Quantity and the Signs of the Times*, *The Crisis of the Modern World*. Cf. also

world are the direct expression of individualism: *hedonism*, meaning unbridled pleasure and success; *utilitarianism*, meaning exploitation and profit; *egalitarianism*, meaning levelling and homogenisation (democracy); *relativism*, meaning free will and sensorial perception; *rationalism*, meaning the primacy of science and of the economy; *progressivism*, meaning pragmatism and mechanism; *vitalism*, meaning the exaltation of life, understood as a vital force, energy, physical vigour, instinct and the will to power.

Vitalism, as a derivative of individualism, is very dangerous, insofar as its expressions are easily confounded for positive and traditional forms, generating confusion in militant youth. By *vitalism* is meant the absolute affirmation of the 'religion of life', almost as if it were an authentic 'superstition' which substitutes the body and the soul — instinct and vital energy — for the Spirit — the essence of being — without creating dangerous deviations. The vital instinct — whose greatest expression is the will to power — is exalted to the point of erasing the difference between the titanic and the heroic. The titan, as opposed to the hero, is caged in his human limits and in his own ego — sentimentalism;[2] his force is the savage and elementary throng of lower nature, the brutal and crude force of the animal and material faculties which tend to overpower consciousness, the inebriation of chaos and of instantaneous sensations. The 'titan' refuses to recognise spiritual reality, discipline and order, and he deludes himself that he has achieved who knows what goals. By contrast, in the hero the

---

J. Evola, *Men Among the Ruins, Revolt Against the Modern World*, and *Ride the Riger*.

2   As Guénon observes in *Symbols of Sacred Science*, sentimentalism is a tendency typical of the modern world, which considers feeling to be the most important part of being, and sensitivity as that which constitutes the sign of its spiritual or merely human elevation. In considering feeling to be superior to intelligence, one engenders the error of exalting the irrational, or, worse yet, the 'infrarational', which leads to that human plane most open to 'suspect' influences. In this regard, Part II of this handbook discusses the risks connected to so-called psychic residues.

experience of disindividualised action, of acting without acting, goes beyond action itself; the hero, evoking in himself a transcendent force, realises an authentic transfiguration and gains the strength to free himself, breaking through the human limit. Thus, the impersonal action transforms itself into rite and Sacred Order.

As J. Evola clarifies: 'But for us it holds, as it always traditionally held, that 'life' is not spirit, and that the spirit is not 'life' — that it is the spirit which gives form to 'life' and that whatever in 'life' presents traits which are truly superior and dominating does not take its origins from 'life' itself, but is the manifestation of the spirit through or by means of life, which amounts to saying, it is something supernatural. Having recognised in these terms the true centre, the gradual shift of one's self-consciousness, one's sense of one's own 'I' from the pole 'life' to the pole 'spirit' is the visible first condition of every true overcoming. Now, today the various voluntarist, atavistic, racistic tendencies act precisely in the opposite direction: they reinforce in every way a purely physical and 'virtual' sensation of the I, they reinforce simultaneously its prison, they create a rigidity, a haughtiness, a sharpened and physicised perception of the will of individuality, of sanity and of power, which are equivalent to so many blockades against inner emancipation. And the circuits remain closed. There lacks any point of reference for the 'self-transforming' of 'intense living' in 'more than living'.

According to the traditional teaching, therefore, the vital forces, representative of the whole of the irrational and sensible influences, must be controlled and subjugated by reason, which, in its turn, must give way to the *awareness of universal principles of order*, which is to say to super-rational consciousness — *intellectual intuition* — whose faculty is Intellect. In this way, the normal order is re-established, without any possibility of confusion: body, soul and spirit.

4.2 THE DOCTRINAL POINTS OF REFERENCE

The absence of any serious knowledge of doctrine, which would be the fruit of a gradual and oriented study, often brings about approximations and confusion. As the exponents of an interpretive 'do-it-yourself-ism', many fall into so-called 'doctrinal exoticism', where what matters is being the most original possible, appropriating figures that have nothing to do with the Traditional style and vision of the world. Such is the case, for instance, with the 'obsession' with socialism, on the part of those who forget that socialism is (also and above all) class warfare and reduction of life to economism, which is to say the antithesis of every integral, organic and corporative conception. Another example is the attempt, which periodically arises, to re-evaluate personages and writers who, however much they may have said interesting things, are from the point of view of example and formation not models for the new generations, which have already been catapulted into an epoch of great mishmash and uncertainties. Let us clarify that such considerations are in no way animated by bigotry or moralism — let all such things be far from us — but simply by the realisation that the militant's formation, insofar as it is the assimilation of a style, is the perfect marriage of doctrine and action. It follows naturally from this, therefore, that *what* one reads and *how* one reads is of importance, given that reading serves to fill the heart with good intentions, and not the brain with sterile notions.

Therefore, given these as our presuppositions, it is preferable to tighten the thread around the points of reference, which are for the most part to be discovered and learned, rather than letting oneself be taken by the mania for originality, thereby nourishing, perhaps unconsciously, a sense of disorientation, whose consequences one always pays in the long run (suffice it to observe what happened to the so-called 'right' the moment it has distanced itself from certain models). No artistic expression, be it from music to art in general, is neutral with regard to the world; every such expression is the manifestation of a form of human approximation to life, to nature, to the cosmos, to the Sacred. One must therefore be very careful when one decides what representatives of these forms should be upheld and disseminated, lest one run the concrete and rather common risk of failing to nourish certainties, and of instead cultivating an anonymous and spineless relativism. One runs the risk, that is to say, of playing the same game as those who are interested in consciously affirming chaos and disorder, as against those who, in an epoch characterised by the same, work with the spirit of sovereign affirmations and absolute negations. The world of Tradition already possesses in itself so many points of reference, so many *examples*, that are by far more convincing and winning. Suffice it to consider the figures of the heroes and of the conquerors of the classical and mythological world, all the way up until our own time, with its protagonists such as Corneliu Zelea Codreanu, Leon Degrelle, Nicolò Giani, Josè Antonio Primo de Rivera, &co.; or again, the work of witnesses to the Tradition such as Julius Evola and René Guénon, to cite only the principal and the most important of these.

And so, is it not the case that this mania for borrowing figures of dubious quality and dignity is testament to the fact that things are in disarray? Is it not the sign, yet again, of a lack of discipline and of structure? Is this, too, not perhaps a form of individualism?

4.3 THE ELITE: HIERARCHY

The ego is the absolute champion (in the negative sense) which makes one forget every form of Roman simplicity, such as ought to spur one to roll up one's sleeves and to set off on the fatiguing climb toward the rediscovery of oneself, of one's own roots, of one's own fathers. The ego is the 'brutal beast' which easily brings one to believe oneself a 'differentiated man', taking for granted that in one's life one has reached important and distinguishing goals. Suffering from a chronic 'strong-man' syndrome, one is unable to comprehend that 'differentiation', or rather 'qualification', is measured and marked in the present, not in the past. Or again, one does not understand that qualification is not to be evaluated only *negatively*, which is to say, in the will to (concretely) reject the modern world and its ideological complex, but also and above all *positively*, in a capacity to effect genuine and real change in the human being.

This step, far from being a given, certifies that qualification cannot be acquired by everyone, it is not within the reach of everyone; qualification must rather be demonstrated with the affirmation of style, or, if you prefer, through example. The simple fact that one holds oneself to belong to a political persuasion or a specific group by itself signifies nothing, and gives one the right to nothing, if not to a simple manifestation of sympathy. To be qualified, it is necessary to form oneself and to better oneself as a man, to make a spiritual, ascetic, aristocratic and heroic vision of life one's own — a vision which is essentially anti-democratic and anti-egalitarian. To affirm, that is, a hierarchical and anti-democratic spirit which translates into the concrete and tangible supremacy of the traditional Values in one's very lifestyle — a sort of daily immanent transcendence.

Hierarchy as value permits the qualification of the man and the community of which he forms a part, since the principle 'to each his own' allows the most courageous, those who most of all incarnate the Traditional Principles, to be the elite, which is to say the central and essential nucleus which influences and confers direction to the whole organisation. The *elite* (the essence) give form to the community and to the movement (the substance), and it is for this reason that the formation which generates qualification represents a priority which we can no longer postpone, if we have at heart the fate of future generations. The elite maintain the living tension, they are the custodians and sentries of the flame; they dedicate themselves to keeping the spiritual force which they bear ever present, for the good of all. Should they falter, there would begin a process of inevitable decadence and distancing from the Centre, and the hierarchy would transform into the well-known hierarchism, through a slow inversion of symbols and distances. And at that point even the head would no longer be a guide responsible for the existential and spiritual growth of the militants, of those who incarnate more than anyone all the Principles of Truth and Justice; not even the head would any longer have the qualification to vitalise them. He would become instead a mere tribune or demagogue.[3]

It is a grave error to think that the strength of a group, of a movement, of a State, is determined from below, or from the so-called quantitative element, since by this path there can be no liberation from the slavery of a democratic, levelling and standardising vision. Every serious attempt to reconquer a social and political space must presuppose the construction and the formation of an elite who are capable of conserving, vitalising and safeguarding the identity and the heredity it has received: the Values of the Tradition.

4.4 MILITANCY AND DESERTION

It often occurs that whoever is not able to give himself form and to acquire a style, attempts to mummify the Tradition and to reduce it to mere parody, judging it an 'incapacitating myth', passive and unrealistic. On the contrary, to negate the viability of the Traditional doctrine means to fail to understand the possibility of making the myth live once more, of actualising it in daily reality and in the surrounding milieu. The inadequacy of incarnating the Values and of rendering them current leads one to confound the Tradition with traditionalism, convention, folklore and nostalgism, and to reduce the principles to an arid conformism, denaturing their vivifying force. This represents

---

3   Let us recall that the head, from the traditional point of view, is the pontifex, the builder of bridges between the sky and the earth — a 'passage' and a middleman who requires the spirit of abnegation, humility, skill and qualification. He is thus far from any form of gratification and personal ambition, or the overweening and patronising attitude which concerns itself with possessing an obsequious and obedient following.

an incapacity to grasp the deep, formative and revolutionary essence of the Tradition, remaining instead entrapped in one's own lack of qualification, in one's own limitless ego. This, unfortunately, is the condition of many 'intellectuals', 'scribes' or 'little professors', or even of many 'rebels' or 'agitators' who, remaining on the plane of beautiful words in the former case or of empty agitations in the latter, measure their adhesion in terms of a cerebral operation or of a fleeting, instinctive and passionate emotion. For both, 'acting' is a flash in the pan, often urged on by the will to do as one pleases, rather than as one ought — action as a form of individual gratification. So much for an 'incapacitating myth'; the truth is that they are flattered by the modern world, and are able to speak of Values alone, not to put them into practice. They are coin-operated rapporteurs who use concepts, terms and models that belong to the world of the Tradition to define ideas and practices that in reality have nothing to do with the Tradition. On the one hand, therefore, we have the academic windbags, those who debate the Tradition in the salons and round tables, almost as if it were an opinion, a philosophy, an ideology or a system of thought; on the other, there are the frenzied purveyors of a sterile activism, who bring misfortunes and disasters upon whomever has the will to build a future. They become, whether consciously or unconsciously, the favoured instruments of Subversion: with their incompetence and their presumption they risk 'neutralising' those who yet feel the impulse to react and to 'rebel' against this system.[4]

However demanding it might be, the difficulty of the objective to be attained does not represent an 'incapacitating myth' for the militant who, with profound realism, is gifted with an inner tension apt to rectify and to overcome his personal limitations. He is conscious that his actions are the result of that which really is (Style), the tangible

---

4   Note how Tradition and *tradire* [Italian for betray — Trans.] share the same etymological root, deriving from the Latin *tradere*, meaning to consign or to transmit. One either transmits, seriously dedicating oneself to that task, or one ends up inevitably betraying that which is supposed to be one's mission.

and concrete manifestation of an *upright man amidst the ruins,* whose example is the necessary and sufficient condition for determining a deep and lasting change.

PART TWO

Vita Est Militare

5. THE FAMILY

5.1 THE DECADENCE OF THE TRADITIONAL MODEL

IN TRADITIONAL SOCIETIES, man already from birth found his first support and the principal point of reference for living a correct existence in his family. He grew and acted following the principles and the rules of a legitimate order, because the family was subject to a hierarchical and organic order, which was realised in the temporal unity between the past (the elders), the present (the parents) and the future (the children). This communitarian structure guaranteed to each person a well-defined role and the possibility of living with respect for amply consolidated models of reference. The familial boundaries, long before the family became a simple natural aggregation founded on blood and relation, affective union or a complex of socio-economic interests, recalled the idea of a 'society of men'. The family was like an Order with its own rules and rites, a unity of divine origin whose members were united by a sense of belonging, of a spiritual character, to the authority of the *pater familias*, founded in turn on a special dignity which naturally conferred respect and loyalty. To the *pater* was connected 'not only the idea of material paternity, but also the idea of a spiritual authority, of a potency, of a majestic dignity',[1] so

---

1   J. Evola, *Revolt Against the Modern World*, Part One, Chapter 6, 'On the Primordial Nature of the Patriciate'.

that, beyond being the military head and the lord of justice, he was also tasked with carrying out the rites and the traditional sacrifices, which each patrician family had the duty of performing. 'The father was precisely the virile priest of the sacred familiar fire, the natural mediator of every efficacious relation with the supersensible, the vivifier par excellence of the mystical force of rite carried out through the substance of fire.'

It is no accident that the attacks brought by the modern world against the institution of the family take as their principal objective that of overturning and eradicating every authority and natural relation. Let us consider the most visible of these attacks, such as divorce, abortion, homosexual adoption, the affirmation of gender ideology, and artificial insemination — examples of how already for some time now a genuine crusade has been proclaimed against the family, thanks to subversive and accommodating legislation. The paternal right, whose distant heritage is to be found in the *Imperium*,[2] has been transformed into simple parental rights, with the consequent confusion of the roles between father and mother.[3] The role of the father and the mother, the simultaneous presence of a masculine and a feminine figure, the model(s) that they provide and the educative support, their respective 'responsibilities' as regards the raising of their children, no

---

2   Imperium derives etymologically from *in paro*, that is to prepare, in the sense of giving life, creating, exercising an authority, commanding. The Imperium is the fullness of sovereign and ordering potency, it is the power which flows from divinity, brought into relation with the virtue and the qualities of the King, in whose person are united political, military, legislative and religious power. It is the divine legitimation of authority, united to the mysterious power (charisma) of the leader, a formative, animating and organising force, capable of imposing order and exercising a direct and irresistible action on the social milieu. Cf. *A Handbook of Traditional Living*, Part One 'The World of Tradition' (London: Arktos Media Ltd., 2010).

3   In this regard, one can see more than single analogy between the authority of the *pater familias* and that of the Rex. Both are founded on the principle of Imperium, the archetype which unites spiritual authority and political power, be it military, legal or social.

longer occupy any normal place in our society, which suffers from a variety of 'identity crises' whose genesis is to be found in the loss of Traditional Values. The family has lost its authentic value, it no longer has a higher meaning, it no longer even performs a social function, since it is an aggregate in which the morality of the *petit bourgeois* reigns; here, relations are conflated with sentimentalism, with friendship, with hypocrisy and with conformism and with a particular lack of communication which is reflected in an equal and corresponding lack of respect. Contemporary society, with its rhythms and its incoherencies, has called into question the knowledge of the elders and their authority; and for the young, as there is no longer a past, it makes little sense to plan for the future.

Returning our gaze to the present, we must mention the results that come of affirming so-called gender ideology, according to which the sexual difference between male and female is a 'cultural' one, or else one that derives 'only' from the type of education imparted on the young, by conditionings which are applied from birth on: I am a man because I have been brought up as a man, I am a woman because I have been brought up as a woman. This work, which is carried out globally, both through the media (campaigns of every kind to condition and manipulate the public opinion) and through norms (the introduction of laws against homophobia and consequent limitations of personal liberty), above all in the so-called Western world, follows from another and broader logic. The unconditional support on the part of the so-called 'powers that be', which is to say those lobbies and foundations which are eternally on the front lines of the affirmation of the globalist ideology (from the 'Rockefeller Foundation' to 'Goldman Sachs', from George Soros' 'Open Societies Foundations' to the 'MacArthur Foundation', to cite but a few) bears witness to how *genderism* is nothing other than the latest instrument in an endless line of such instruments, bent on affirming that man who is without fatherland, without history, without religion and without sex — who is homogenised and easy to manipulate according to one's taste. To the contrary, the difference between man and woman is of a substantial type (that is, it is not only morphological but also spiritual) and the polarity of the sexes is an indispensable value for normal social functioning.[4]

This is an indisputable indication of how the 'old' identity and sense of belonging deriving from the institution of the family have now fallen beneath a violent and fierce assault, aimed at the obliteration of one more obstacle along the terrible and disquieting road toward the affirmation of that amorphous and erased man, the perfect citizen of the new global government.

5.2 THE MILITANT AND RELATIONS WITH PARENTS

Despite the fact that the choice to be a militant is not always hindered by one's parents, it can sometimes occur that this relationship is not always serene and calm, and that, especially at the beginning of the path one has chosen, there may be many misunderstandings. Militancy does indeed represent a 'new life' which demands breaking with the routine and the habits which one has hitherto followed. This change, almost always unexpected, is accentuated by the enthusiasm of its early moments and can be accompanied by poor school reports or by certain exuberant attitudes which, almost always, alarm parents; and so they, not comprehending what is happening to their child, attempt to apply pressure in a variety of ways, following the instinct of an erring sense of protection. Here is the most difficult moment for a young militant, who faces the necessity of resisting this 'encircling manoeuvre', based as it is on sentimental and conformistic appeals: one's affects, the relationship with one's girlfriend, a good job, one's career and the security entailed in a normal life, are the sirens which

---

4   We defer the reader to an excellent and exhaustive investigation of this theme in the study of E. Perucchetti and G. Marletta, *Unisex: La creazione dell'uomo senza identità* (Bologna. Arianna editrice: 2014).

would beguile a man back to ordinariness. However, to resist does not have to require the degeneration of familial relations or a rigidity in one's personal position. To close oneself off to one's parents is actually an immature attitude, indicative that one is not yet capable of confronting and managing the problems that reality poses, and thoroughly understanding one's own existential choice. On the contrary, to be conscious of one's role as a responsible child, both with regard to oneself and with regard to one's parents, permits a mitigation of the situation, and brings one to look at one's duties, one's studies, one's work, one's girlfriend, not to speak of one's relations with one's own family, from a different point of view — the point of view which considers these things to be the occasion for true existential growth, which is to be conquered anew each day. Through the rectification of one's own life, the militant can become the point of reference even for his parents, as a man capable of assuming his own responsibilities and able to see his duties through.

The Traditional path imposes equilibrium and the capacity to imbue a still green personality with character, and to have done with the role of a spoiled child, smothered with the loving care of his parents, ungrateful for the sacrifices of others and living as a parasite. Through a responsible and ever more mature attitude, one must make one's parents understand that one has grown up, not because one stays out late at night, but because one has become a man capable of performing one's duties before claiming one's rights. Then it will be a matter of course that one be accepted for what one is; then it will be possible, despite the inevitable resistance put up by this or that sense of maternal possession, to cut the 'umbilical cord'.

5.3 MARRIAGE

The decision to marry should not be made with superficiality and haste. In order to form a family, one must reflect, beforehand and not afterwards, on responsibility, duties, responsibilities and the prospects brought by living one's life together with another person. It is important to keep the value of marriage clearly in mind as a sacrament; one must clearly see the meaning of the rite and the influences that it unleashes,[5] so as to avoid its transforming into a kind of mere convention. In this regard, suffice it to observe what occurs nowadays in many Western countries, where the choice to marry is not made with requisite consciousness and responsibility, and divorce has therefore become a true constant. Indeed, while from a Traditional point of view there is nothing standing *a priori* against the dissolution of a marriage,[6] on the other hand the futile motives which often characterise divorce in our day cannot be accepted; it is almost as if today there prevailed the logic that, once one has been married, there is always a possible 'way out', a loophole in one's responsibility.

The militant who wishes to marry knows how important the choice of spouse is; this is the person with whom he will share the fortunes of his life, creating the spiritual communion necessary for their respective inner growth. Beyond affinity in character, it is essential to have a

---

5   'In the world of the Tradition, nothing was considered more useful than the spiritual influences that rite could activate with its necessitating action. ... The father was the virile priest of the sacred familial flame. ... The communal rite thus constituted the true cement of the familial unity and often even of the *gens*. ... Rite, more than blood, united; and rite separated as well.' Cf. J. Evola, *Revolt Against the Modern World*, Part One, Chapter 6, 'On the Primordial Nature of the Patriciate and Chapter 7, 'On Spiritual Virility'. It is important that the union of marriage be sanctioned by a true religious rite, excluding folkloristic 'do-it-yourself' weddings or the secular conventions of mere civic marriage.

6   Recall the many traditions that allowed 'repudiation' on the part of the husband or voluntary distancing on the part of the wife — rare and special cases, however, which did not undermine the general principle of familial unity.

person at one's side who is capable of understanding and sharing one's choices, a person with whom, beyond enthusiasm and sentiment, one can build a formative project whose solid foundations stand on love, dignity, friendship and the respect for family roles. These last, therefore, must be defined and verified beforehand, in awareness that the inebriation of being in love is followed by the duties and responsibilities of a communal life. Moreover, given the present times, one must ensure the economic stability of one's family through a stable job, such as can guarantee tranquillity in facing the costs that a family normally entails. A couple who marry with a dowry of reciprocal love alone (love which has yet, incidentally, to be tested) might make the subject matter of a nice romantic film, but not of the modern reality of a family with children to maintain.

For the militant, therefore, marriage is another trial for getting to know oneself and for proving oneself, an experience in growth and responsibility, in which the spiritual union between man and woman is elevated beyond the naturalistic and sentimental plane.[7] This marks a communion of intentions and of destiny, capable of sublimating and subsuming the differences of the persons involved, so that these differences become a fount of wealth and enhancement, rather than an impediment or an element of attrition.

---

7   'We can admit at once a higher idea of matrimony, as a sacred and indissoluble union not by one's word, but by one's deed. This kind of union is however conceivable only in exceptional cases, in the cases in which there is present, from the very beginning, that absolute, almost heroic dedication of one person to the other, in life and beyond life; this was known in more than one traditional civilisation, wherein one finds examples even of spouses who considered it natural to perish themselves after the death of their husbands.' Cf. J. Evola, *Ride the Tiger*, Chapter 27, 'Marriage and the Family'.

5.4 PARENTING

The birth of a child should not be the result of an accident or an adventure, but must be chosen, desired and conscious. The sexual act which aims toward procreation is a creative action, the fateful moment in which the spirit incarnates in a new life. It is no accident that in many traditions there is talk of the 'child of duty', who is consecrated to the divine,[8] and understood as a responsibility toward one's ancestors rather than simply the venting of pleasure dictated by one's instincts. The very idea of Tradition is inherent in the transmission of life from parents to children, a heredity not only of the biological, physical or psychic kind, but also of a spiritual and transcendent order. To become parents is a responsibility one assumes both toward oneself and toward others, a choice which is demanding and wonderful at the same time, and which necessitates appropriate evaluations in order to avoid later delusions or frustrations. It should indeed not be forgotten that the conditions of modern society are absolutely unfavourable to raising a child in a healthy and balanced way, given the absence of educational models and supports.

All the more reason, then, that it is fundamentally important to apply the right educative methods with respect to one's children — methods in which both parents carry out their proper function with severity and comprehension, avoiding a relation of friendship with their

---

8   The son is 'he who must take up and nourish the supernatural element of the bloodline, the liberation of the ancestor; who must receive and transmit "strength, life, stability". Never before as in the modern world has all of this seemed an insipid fantasy; men, rather than possessing sex, are possessed by it, flinging themselves drunkenly here and there, utterly losing the ability to know what might ignite in their embraces, or to see the demon that woefully toys with them through their search for pleasure and their passion — so much so, that without them knowing anything about it — beyond it being often against their will — a new being sooner or later arises accidentally from one of these nights, often as an intruder, without any spiritual continuity.' J. Evola, *Revolt Against the Modern World*, Part One, Chapter 21, 'The Decline of the Superior Races'.

child which would permit it to indulge in every caprice. A father and a mother must be examples for their children, models who help them to confront the trials of life with courage and faith. Attention regarding *what* one's children ought to learn should go hand in hand with *how* they ought to learn it, putting emphasis on the value of commitment and sacrifice, stimulating the search for values and for virtues, helping to form their identity as early as adolescence, freeing them from prejudices and from conditionings, instilling in them the sense of honour and respect for authority. A father, with the help of maternal love and affection, must furnish his son with a code of behaviour such as to induce him to develop his own orientations in daily existence, favouring the formation of character, that he does not become subsumed by others but remains ever himself. In this respect, some help might come from exercise connected to certain disciplines which can stimulate curiosity, the confrontation with one's own limits, exhaustion, sacrifice, fear: trekking and mountain climbing, for example, or in any case a great many activities connected to nature, or also boxing and martial arts — activities which affirm the spirit of the combatant and respect for his adversary — or again, rugby, in which one discovers team spirit and the principle of abnegation.

However, it would be well not to delude oneself: it is theirs, and theirs alone, to decide whether or not to inherit a spiritual patrimony or a specific vision of the world — a choice which, conditions permitting, will be made in the right moment.

5.5 RESPONSIBLE CHOICES

The final frontiers of ethics have been shattered and scientific experimentation today no longer obeys any rule, if not that of an insatiable desire for profit. For many modern scientists, man is now considered an agglomeration of cells acting within well-defined structures, governed by more or less automatic chemical reactions. While it is impossible for us to give an exhaustive consideration of this matter here, it is nonetheless necessary to emphasise certain questions of a general character, in which respect for the delicacy and dramatical nature of certain choices stands side by side with awareness of the subversive if not criminal and greedy logic behind them.

For example, in the practice of harvesting and transplanting organs, the human being has become a machine whose parts can be substituted and interchanged at will. Accompanied by a constant persuasive ('awareness-building') campaign, the so-called organ donation masks, in a conniving way and with 'humanitarian' aims, wide-ranging economic interests. Indeed, we are never told what truly happens: namely, that organ harvesting is effected always and exclusively on persons in coma, unconscious, whose reactions to the suffering produced by the harvest are impeded by paralysing pharmaceuticals or by anaesthetics. In this same context, it is well to recall how those who wish to protect their refusal to be donors must openly express this, since the present legislation holds to the rule that silence means assent: those who do not express their will are considered voluntary donors.[9] Man is something more than a collection of organs that carry out vital functions without having any connection to one another apart from the merely physiological. The organs are part of an organic whole that operates in harmony: the perfect symbiosis of body, soul and spirit.[10] The same holds also in the case of blood

9   The right to opposition can manifest if the living person is conscious and documents his opposition, for example through a will or a signed declaration, or through relatives who present written opposition within the period of a false certification of cerebral death. This does not hold in those cases in which it has been documented that the sick person is a donor and has not documented a change of mind through any further signed declaration. For more information, visit the site www.antipredazione.org. Moreover, it should be noted that, even as this book is being issued, the Rome has established that it is possible to register one's will regarding the donation of organs and tissues simultaneously as one requests or renews one's identity card. For more information, visit the site www.comune.roma.it.

10   To remove an organ from a body in order to implant it into another brings about the unbalancing of these dynamics, a mixing of various energetic aspects

donation and the transfusions which follow from it — a 'humanitarian' practice which is very common and much propagandised, in
which it is forgotten that the blood is the vehicle of specific subtle
energies — the vital force — and that it characterises not only a specific
stock, but also the person himself.

Beyond the question of transplants, abortion also deserves special
consideration, as this is a problem which a young militant could easily
confront himself. On account of an obliging legislation but, above all,
of a society which has completely lost any sense for the meaning of
life, the killing of a child is tolerated today simply because one has
committed an error or has taken matters lightly; rationalisations of a
scientific character are adduced regarding the nature of the embryo
which is, however, is a full-fledged human being already from conception.[11] Abortion, therefore, is the voluntary homicide of an innocent
and defenceless human being.[12]

The cases highlighted here are examples of how the militant must
approach contemporary society and its machinations, toward the end

---

of two persons. The subtle anatomy, moreover, is forever altered and modified.

11   As is demonstrated by scientific research itself, the embryo contains within it
the entire genome, which is to say the structure which carries within itself, as if
in a kind of memory, the essential information for the gradual formation and
development of the human individual. It is the genome which distinguishes the
uniqueness of the embryo, which differentiates it from every other and which
confers upon it its identity. The genome possesses three extremely important
properties which characterise the process of development of the embryo: co-
ordination, the process of development of the embryo, beginning from when
it is a zygote and continuing from there; continuity, or the execution of the
uninterrupted process of growth from beginning to end; and graduality, the
development from simpler forms to more complex forms. This implies that
identity is present already from the start, and the only thing that changes is the
gradual realisation of the final form.

12   A further consideration should be made as regards Ru486, known as the
'morning-after pill', which still more encourages the irresponsibility of the
woman with respect to abortion, as it can permit her to avoid the risks attached
to surgical intervention. On this subject, see also P. Rauti, Perché no all'aborto,
Raido, Rome 1999.

of reawakening in himself the capacity to reason in an autonomous and independent manner on the various forms of manipulation which surround him. On the one hand, he must be conscious of how these phenomenologies represent the product of moral relativism and of the individualist morality underpinning science and modern culture, and on the other hand he must make an effort to investigate beyond sentimental and humanitarian appearances, toward the end of discovering concealed economic and speculative interests. All apocalyptic predictions or catastrophic visions aside, we live in a time in which there already exist instruments through which, in the name of profit and of other low motivations, many individuals are prepared to destroy life.

In conclusion, if the complexity of certain dramatic choices should not frighten us, at the same time they cannot be lived through 'light-heartedly'. In the face of certain decisions, upon which the life of a loved one might depend, one must not reason in an obtuse or sanctimonious way, getting tangled up in a 'Jehovah's witness' type morality, but, at the same time, one must not fail to step toward a critical spirit, toward an evaluation oriented around the vision of the world founded on the Sacred, for which life has an above all qualitative value. It is not easy for the militant to live through such things, and there are no pre-fabricated formulae permitting him to reach the best decision; however, one thing is certain, even in these moments — or rather, above all in these moments: it is necessary to take inspiration from the criteria of Truth and Justice, and not only from exclusively sentimental factors.

6. RELATIONS BETWEEN THE SEXES

6.1 THE NATURE OF THE SEXES

THE NATURE OF THE SEXES, beyond mere morphological differences, affects also the psychic and spiritual characteristics of a man and a woman, and its identity embraces all those aspects of their respective personalities. As Guido de Giorgio observes, 'if we schematically and symbolically reduce the principles of masculine and feminine to two wedges, to two angles (which corresponds exactly to the physiological brutalism of the sexual function) we have two cusps inserted into the same centre: one *active*, the other *passive*; one *emissive*, the other *receptive*; one *creator*, the other *conserver*; one *fecundator,* the other *producer*; one *germigenous* the other *germiferous*'.[1] In antiquity, in attempts to explain the sexes, recourse was made to the myth of the Androgyne, the bisexual being, who in its unity is perfect, incorruptible and immortal, to the point that the very gods, fearing it, decided to divide it into two parts, one male and the other female. From the division of the andogryne, man has inherited the pure transcendent and supernatural principle — the *being* — associated with the symbols of the sun, of the sky and of fire;

---

1   G. de Giorgio, *Prospettive della Tradizione*, edizioni Il Cinabro, Catania 1999, p. 91.

while woman has inherited the natural principle — the *becoming* — associated with the moon, with the earth and with water. The moon is the sacred representation of becoming: it waxes, wanes and disappears only to be reborn; it is the manifestation of rhythm and of measure. Lunar time is a cosmic and biological time, upon which the tides and various agricultural activities depend (as for example the sowing of crops) and it is connected to the periods of menstruation and of female fecundity. The male element, on the other hand, is associated with the symbol of sky-rain, and thus of the fecundating element; it transmits form-energy to the female element, symbol of the earth and of the fecundated principle, thus conferring life upon it.[2]

The nature of man is stable, complete and sufficient unto itself, while that of woman is more versatile and is agitated by desire and passion. Indeed, in all traditions the attitude of change has brought about the representation of woman as possessing a double meaning: on the one hand as a trial and a 'danger', on the other as the vivifying principle of power. This principle is dangerous if it remains mere carnal seduction, a yielding to the passions and to the instincts; but it is the symbol of life when it assumes the transfiguring power which must be conquered and mastered by the hero. In this last case, passion and need 'disappear', not by their repression in a forced abstinence, but because they are satisfied and absorbed in a superior union: sexual energy is converted into spiritual energy. Woman, in this case, becomes the incarnation of a transfiguring spirituality, in which *eros* — love — represents one possibility of participation in the higher forms of being.

---

2   Water is the representation from which all forms are born. In the waters are found the two faces of becoming: generation and destruction, just as for 'being reborn', in an initiatic sense, one must first pass through the phase of dissolution.

6.2 POLARITY AND COMPLEMENTARITY OF THE SEXES

Give that differences in body are nothing other than the manifestation of an interior difference, man and woman each represent a specific way of being, of living and of relating to the world. This difference must be recognized and affirmed, without admixture and diminution, as the considerations of Otto Weininger, taken up by Evola:

> [A]ll 'normal' sexuality derives from the psycho-physical states engendered by the opposition of two principles operating like magnetic poles, the masculine and the feminine. I am speaking here of 'masculine' and 'feminine' *in an absolute sense,* meaning two principles governing what is ultimately a metaphysical — and not just a physical — order. These principles may be present to widely varying degrees in men and women. Indeed, in real life 'absolute' men and women are found just about as often as the abstract triangle of pure geometry. We rather find beings in whom either the masculine quality is predominant ('men') or the feminine one is ('women'), but in whom the opposite quality is never completely absent. The basic law of sexual attraction, already presented by Plato and Schopenhauer, and later clearly formulated by Weininger, is that sexual attraction in its most typical forms stems from the encounter between a man and a woman such that the sum of the masculine and feminine parts contained in each makes up an absolute man and an absolute woman. To illustrate this with an example, a man who is three quarters man and one quarter woman will find himself irresistibly, magnetically attracted to a woman who is three quarters woman and one quarter man: for the sum in this case would be precisely one absolute man and one absolute woman, combined into one. This law applies to every intense, deep and 'elementary' eroticism between the two sexes; it does not concern degraded, watered-down, bourgeois or merely 'ideal' and sentimental forms of love and sexuality.[3]

For their individualities to be completed, man and woman must come into relation with one another: when their union is perfected, both of them become 'integral beings' in their fullness, and the sexual

---

3   See *The Bow and the Club* (London: Arktos Media Ltd., 2019), pp. 17–18.

act, imbued with a magical and spiritual force, sublimates the mere instinctual manifestation. Once all of this has been lost, and every higher value associated with sex has been abandoned, the impromptu pursuit of pleasure inevitably predominates, transforming woman into an object to conquer and man into a libidinous being, 'all sex and no brain'.[4]

It is a given how sex represents a force which influences and conditions many individual acts, involving the private sphere of fantasy, of the imagination and of character — a sphere which it is difficult, if not impossible, to penetrate by means of simple rationality.[5] In general, such a confrontation is particularly educational for the militant: to feel compulsion vibrating and instinct rising unstoppably makes for an important trial, so as to learn how to manage oneself and how to control an overpowering and irrational force, to have an active and affirmative attitude in the face of experiences which easily induce one to lose one's lucidity. Moreover, the sexual act is a moment of mutual exchange of energies and influences, which can cause interior upheaval and of leaving an invisible sign in the depths of being. This, far from being a sterile moralism, should be kept in mind above all in the case of so-called 'casual sex' or, particularly, during the period of menstruation. In that period, the sexual act should be totally avoided, because (hygienic considerations aside) it is a peculiar period, intimately connected to the feminine nature, whose intimacy and emotionality

---

4   Nowadays, moreover, the abundance of sex, which is available at every hour and in every place, has led to its banalisation and a consequent loss of potentiality, to the point that so great an accessibility has led fantasy to overcome reality and virtuality to be preferred to experience. It is ever more difficult to experience a natural sexual act without physical or psychological difficulties.

5   'The force of sex is at the very root of the living individual, and whoever believes he can truly repress it deludes himself. At most, he can repress its direct manifestations, with the result that they will go to nourish those phenomena of a neurotic and fractured existence, upon which modern psychoanalysis has thrown even too much light'. J. Evola, *Metaphysics of Sex*, Edizioni Mediterranee, Rome 1996, p. 249.

is involved in the release of energies from which men ought to carefully preserve themselves. In ancient times, sexual acts were severely prohibited during the menstrual cycle, and whoever was overcome by desire, joining with a woman in this state was thought to have committed an unnatural act; more than that, he was considered foolish and vulgar and on the verge of losing his wisdom and vital force.[6]

6.3 WOMAN: GIFT AND DEDICATION

From the point of view of formation and realisation, man and woman, in function of their difference, possess specific routes toward the approximation of the Spiritual Principle. In this regard, Julius Evola recalls that in the principal forms for approximating the value of 'being by oneself', Action and Contemplation:

> the Warrior (the Hero) and the Ascetic — are the two fundamental types of pure virility. In symmetry to these, there are also two types for feminine nature. Woman realises herself as woman, she elevates herself to the same level as man the Warrior and man the Ascetic, insofar as she is Lover or Mother. As these forms represent bipartition of one and the same ideal strain, just as there is an active heroism, so there is a negative heroism; there is the heroism of absolute affirmation and there is that of absolute devotion — the one might be as luminous as the other, the one might be as rich as the other in the fruits of overcoming and liberation, when it is lived with purity, as an offering. Precisely this differentiation in the heroic strain determines the distinctive characteristic of the paths to completion for man and for woman as types. The gesture of the Warrior and the Ascetic who

---

6   In the ancient Indo-European code *Manavadharmaçastra* it is stated that man 'even if he is outside of himself [with desire] must not have sexual relations with a woman who is menstruating; he must not even lie in the same bed as such a one. A man who has sexual relations with a menstruating woman loses his wisdom, his brilliant energy, his strength, his sight and his longevity'. For this reason, during the menstrual period, women were separated into designated places, so that they would not 'contaminate' the other members of their family and of society, and even conversation was prohibited to them. Cf. Manavadharmaçastra, *The Laws of Manu* IV, 40, 41 and 57.

affirm a life which is beyond life — the one a means of pure action and the other a means of pure detachment — find their corresponding gesture in that woman who wholly gives herself to another being, her being entirely for another being, be he her beloved man (the type of the Lover — aphroditic woman) or her child (the type of the Mother — Demetric woman), finding in this being the sense of her life, her joy, her justification.[7]

The task of the masculine element, the principle which qualifies and orders it, is to transmit the form and the essence of things. The task of the feminine element is to incarnate this form and to give it life. 'Between the seed (creative masculine power) and the womb (feminine power), it is said that the most important is the seed, since the progeny of all beings is characterized by the characteristics of the seed. That which grows in a field prepared in the right season, manifesting its proper specific qualities, is of the same kind as the seed which has been planted. Indeed, it is said that this earth is the eternal womb of the creatures, but in the things that it makes grow none of the qualities of the womb are manifested. In this world, indeed, when the farmers sow the earth in the right season, even in one and the same field, with seeds of various kinds, these grow according to their proper nature. ... It never happens that one sows one kind of seed and another kind grows; whatever seed is sown, it is that which grows.'[8]

The realisation of woman is achieved when her devotion to a man is absolute, or else when her offer comes with 'simplicity and purity',[9] without hidden agendas and personal interests. Woman is able to give order to her life through a love which 'gives without asking', a dedication which is developed without any passionate or possessive support.

7   J. Evola, *Revolt Against the Modern World*, Part One, Chapter 20, 'Man and Woman'.

8   Manavadharmaçastra, *The Laws of Manu*, IX, 35, 36, 37 and 40.

9   It is doubtless that in the case of a man who is deprived of adequate qualification, and therefore who is unable to respond to his proper role, the pure and active devotion of a woman for him assumes a character of such a heroism that she is rendered his superior.

This is not a question of self-nullification so much as of a conscious and pure offering, of achieving what is right without expecting anything in return, of striving to render a couple's bonds ever stronger. To be a militant woman, therefore, means to open oneself to love as the manifestation of the Universal Principle — a love which gains in transcendent and extraordinary value the moment it translates into pure devotion to another (whether man or child) and in giving oneself in an impersonal way. If the gift, as such, requires no recompense, no measure, that 'love' which is the fruit of possession on the contrary permits no opening of the transcendent type for woman, who remains tied to exclusively human and sentimentalistic horizons. Womanly devotion stands side by side with the impersonal action of man with respect to the Idea. His duty is to be each day a warrior worthy of the name; her unconditional *fides* is capable of sublimating sentiment and triumphing over every egoism and vanity, affirming a love which supersedes human boundaries, elevating itself over and transcending them. The limit resides in the subtle line separating conscious devotion, whose faithfulness has no need to ask any recompense in man, from maniacal possession, which binds him to her interest. Devotion confers substance on and elevates a woman, while possession degrades her so far as to finally denature and skew every relationship.

To be a woman in contemporary society is an exacting challenge which requires sacrifice — a path of formation and rectification, parallel and complementary to that of the man who aspires to differentiate himself. A woman can accept and bear this only if she makes a hard and conscious existential turnabout. For those who wish to take up this challenge, the traditional woman may serve as an example — she who was capable of offering in a way that went beyond the sentimental and human plane, of giving herself with simplicity, of not living for herself but for the other, of a form which was capable of manifesting all of its heroism, participating in the Sacred Order.

6.4 RECTIFICATION OF THE SEXES

To re-establish the natural order, man and woman must rectify certain typical attitudes, restoring a relationship of 'camaraderie' founded on a style of loyalty, clarity, sincerity and inner liberty, lived without subtext or sentimental breakdowns: the mutual compensation and interpenetration of two different ways of being. On this basis, even sex will come to assume a spiritual meaning.

Such a task necessitates a great effort on the part of the woman and, at the same time, it will render the man responsible for the assumption of his proper duties. Against the egalitarian and levelling tendency of the contemporary world, the woman must seek her own identity through authentically 'being woman' and, without aping man in attitudes and roles, must exert herself in reawakening the interior tension of devotion and of giving in an absolute and active way. 'A virtuous wife [woman] must constantly serve [venerate] her husband [her man] as if he were a god, even if he should behave badly [not following the straight way], abandons himself to concupiscence [gives himself to other loves] and is lacking in any good quality [qualification]. Divided [from their men], women cannot sacrifice, nor initiate a vow or a fast; it is because a woman obeys her husband that she is glorified in heaven. A virtuous wife must never do anything which displeases her husband'.[10]

For man, on the other hand, the path to rectification and qualification according to the Principles of Tradition assumes the double aspect of the virtuous rediscovery of himself, and of aid and support of his consort. He must exert himself to restore the order in his existence, reappropriating to himself the principle which characterises him, so that woman might find in him a point of reference and a support to realise herself, without imitating him or feeling herself crippled for this reason. Only in this way can woman once more have her own identity and a clear dignity, the true dimension of her nature which

---

10   Manavadharmaçastra, *The Laws of Manu*, V, 154–156.

has nothing to do with the grievances brought by the feminist stereotype. On the other hand, a man without qualification represents the inevitable corollary of a disharmonic relationship, in which the roles are compromised and inverted. For example, a man must avoid those disorderly attitudes brought about by morbid forms of attachment (possession and jealousy), such as are characteristic of that man who feels lost without his woman beside him (or without a woman beside him); likewise he must avoid those attitudes typical of the 'little dictator' who masks and compensates for his own interior deficiencies and shortcomings by imposing a force which is, rather than the reflection of his virility in the spiritual sense, simply the deplorable manifestation of his insolence.[11] Such men demonstrate that they are incapable of fueling and grasping the 'magic' of woman; and such relationships remain exclusively on a physical and amicable plane (which is to say, they remain purely sexual and sentimental), without any possibility of a higher order and an effectively qualifying union.

The more that a man succeeds in dedicating himself to the task of reconquering his lost virility, thus assuming his proper responsibilities, the more a woman will succeed in helping him, in standing at his side, and in rediscovering a natural femininity and a charm which is totally lacking in pretence.

---

11 It is normally the woman who must seek a man and not the other way around; it is she who must feel herself attracted by his virility, since it is the woman who realises herself in love and not man, whose realisation comes in a different domain.

7. CONFRONTATION WITH THE WORLD OF WORK

7.1 WORK AS PAIN

IN THE ANCIENT WORLD, work was associated with the concept of pain (πόνος), with a dark fatigue determined by need, which bound the individual, the slave, to material necessity; the free man, on the other hand, though he might engage in some business, was always attentive to the quality of his action, which was never disconnected from a very clear qualification and personal vocation. He was the *artifex* who acted in a higher sense. Not accidentally, the functions of the ancient corporations of art and trades took as their principal characteristics the anagogic element, that is, an element which was capable of drawing them toward the heights.

In the course of the centuries, work gradually transformed into the alter upon one sacrificed one's life, bounding it to the rhythms and logic of production. Work became an ethical imperative; the working class was ever more glorified and praised, and man's principal aim was no longer to free himself, but to model his existence on the necessity of work, losing sight of every higher reference point. Today, man lives to work; he sells himself, his own working strength or his own ingenuity, just as a prostitute would do. To be ever more productive (and consumptive), working rhythms have become ever faster, bringing about the rise of the so-called disorders of contemporary man, such as anguish and emotive stress.

Modern work has nothing ethical about it and nothing natural; it does not generate dynamics of solidarity, but only of competition and conflict and negation of every social harmony. As has already been observed, individualistic man is the product of all of this, shrewd and cynical, faithful to the motto that 'time is money' and moulded by the idea that man acts usefully only when working: the whole of life is exclusively catalysed by the economic and material factor and by the well-known formula *produce/consume/die*. Even one's interests outside of work are transformed into recreation and repose, ever and always as a function of work, of the need to start again tomorrow more productively than ever. The individual, amorphous and entrapped in a diabolical machine, becomes the perfect bourgeois man, transforming every social relationship into a relationship of the contractual kind: life itself becomes a contract, a giving and a having, in the search for egotistical profit, regulated and imposed by the laws of the economy.

Society, consequently, is founded on interests, bereft of any solidary limit deriving from one's belonging to a community (a grouping of families), to a land (to be defended and valorised), to a fatherland (the land of one's fathers), or to an Idea (such as might unite, fortify and give rise to heroes) — and all of this toward the end of that total uprooting which is being carried out today on all fronts. This is an absolutely unstable equilibrium, still more unstable in the face of the growing social and economic crises now underway, which is dominated by a sense of precariousness, as testimony to the fact that the modernist and progressivist ideology is no longer capable of guaranteeing even one of its sacrosanct pillars.

7.2 ERNST JÜNGER'S WORKER

In his book *The Worker*,[1] Ernst Jünger attempted to overcome the absurd and aberrant world of modern work characterised by the so-called 'mass production', which does not concede space for quality since it produces identical objects, deprived of every intrinsic value beyond their material components, and by simple mechanical exercise bereft of interior tension: in a climate of anonymity, the worker, automised and computerised, performs his task of identical and repetitive gestures.

The Jüngerian worker and labourer is opposed to this world; he represents a new type of human who acts with absolute realism and impersonality. He is the expression of a way of being forged in the lacerating experience of war; in times of peace, he renews this way of being as if it were a potential and realisable interior liberation. Since the value of honour has vanished, the worker acts in his company like a soldier in wartime; he confronts a ruthless enemy who takes no prisoners, facing this enemy's technology and its elementary force, which is represented by the steel of the machines. He acts with detachment and with absolute dedication, he accepts the danger as a challenge, destroying every shred of idealism and romanticism proper to bourgeois society. The Jüngerian worker is the artificer of his own life and no longer a simple gear in the chain of production-consumption.

Ernst Jünger does not seek to affirm a vision of the economic kind, but rather to build a new kind of human — a man to whom every kind of individualism and utilitarianism is alien, a man gifted with a heroic realism, and a new civilisation capable of opposing itself to bourgeois conformism. However, contrary to all expectations, such a break in level was not actuated historically, and it is unthinkable that it might become the premise of a superior civilisation in the

---

1   Cf. Ernst Jünger, *Der Arbeiter. Herrschaft und Gestalt* (1932), and Julius Evola, *L'operaio nel pensiero di Ernst Jünger* (Rome: Edizioni Mediterranee, 1998). [Neither of these works has been translated into English. — Trans.]

near future. Indeed, for something of the kind to occur, the human substance itself would have to be radically different, which is to say, gifted with a rectified and formed style which is able to see beyond exclusively social grievances or exclusively material considerations. The industry workers crammed into their alienating assembly lines, the employees mouldering in some anonymous office, the rampant managers of some stars-and-stripes multinational corporation, but also the unemployed who protest in the streets to defend their jobs, are all in any case the various faces of one and the same coin: the principal aspiration is bourgeois hedonism. At bottom, as has already been observed, the dominant sentiment of contemporary society is envy, where everyone claims for himself the rights of the other, in a continual struggle for survival.

Therefore, until man has freed himself from the individualism and utilitarianism which condemn him to an inhuman work, the intuitions of Jünger will remain such, without any possibility of practical application. Indeed, before evaluating the value of technology and progress, or of the irruption of the masses into history, or of the exaltation of work as spiritual elevation, man must first find himself once more through the formation and the verification of his self.

7.3 COMMITTING ONESELF: STUDYING OR WORKING

For many, rebelling against the bourgeois society is synonymous with living 'in the now', refusing to study or to work or to give an account for one's commitments and responsibilities. Such people take as their model the 'rebel', despite the fact that behind this pseudo-revolutionary there is hidden, in most cases, a misfit incapable of changing the reality which surrounds him; his 'revolt' is nothing other than a flight from himself into sterile agitation.

The militant of the Tradition, on the contrary, opposes to the bourgeois ideal of convenience and of mediocrity the 'warrior' style of that man who confronts life with enthusiasm and awareness, the revolutionary lucidity of those who do not withdraw in the face of the trials which life presents. Study and work are commitments that must be honoured and realised, not only so as to guarantee a man a self-sufficient life, but above all because they are instruments by which to verify his own militant qualification. During the scholastic period, the militant must identify what his future job might be and must exert himself toward realising this in the briefest amount of time possible and with the greatest possible results, without procrastinating in his tasks out of thoughtlessness or some other cause. It is absolutely wrong to think that life's problems will somehow be resolved by the intervention of one's family, by fortune or by friends, and it is wrong to slacken in one's efforts, finally blaming others or society. Even in the realm of work, the militant must demonstrate that he is trustworthy, competent and efficient in his proper field of action and competency, aware of the hierarchy of his own existential interests and of the energies he must bring to bear. He remains ever a man of style, not attracted by easy earnings, conscious that a good occupation is the instrument for conducting a dignified life and, at the same time, for contributing to the militant cause.[2] His truly revolutionary spirit, his practical and realistic attitude considers work experience a further field of action for

---

2   Let it be recalled that within an organic community each contributes according to his own competencies and possibilities. Given that each activity in favour of the idea requires certain sums of money, whoever works must contribute with a tenth of his income to the self-financing of the activity, while whoever studies must give a contribution which is lesser in economic terms but greater in terms of time and energy. Moreover, the student must be aware that his true task, in the future, is a professional qualification that can be made available to the community, and in support of the project that this community advances: workers, labourers, craftsmen, farmers, free professionals, specialists of various kinds, etc. are indispensable figures in an organic and truly revolutionary context. Cf. *A Handbook of Traditional Living*, Part Two: The Front of Tradition, Chapter 12, 'The Operative Unit' (London: Arktos Media Ltd., 2010).

explicating his militancy, twenty-four hours a day and without pause, with constancy and strength of spirit, responsibility and method.[3]

To consider modern work alien to a Traditional vision certainly must not constitute an excuse for the militant. In fact, poor performance in work or in study are conditions that do not marry with the warrior spirit; an entirely different interior predisposition is necessary for such spirit.

7.4 CRAFTSMANSHIP AND FARMING

For the militant who commences on a journey of interior rectification, craftsmanship and agriculture, as compared to other kinds of working activity, have certain advantages. Rather than a 'mystical' flight into the green of nature, toward the rediscovery of the myth of the Rousseauian noble savage — as, for instance many hippy communities attempted — farming and craftsmanship are excellent instruments in the quest for and awareness of oneself.

Indeed, according to the traditional interpretation, by conferring upon material a determinate form, the craftsman or farmer (*artifex*) can analogously act on their own interior consciousness, transforming themselves. Work becomes an art capable of expressing the personality of man, a means fit for improvement and spiritual reinforcement, a daily method for interior overcoming. Through an action which becomes 'ritual', one affirms the analogy between that which one does and the possibility of freeing oneself from human limits, so as to attempt to elevate oneself to the sacred dimension. The artist, through the aspiration to transform raw material in accordance with natural rhythms, and in harmony with the cosmos, is able to infuse this material with life and form, conferring an order, participating, in

---

3   Consider the daily confrontation with a series of attitudes and human types in the restricted space of an office, where gossip, jealousy, presumption, neuroticism, falsity or servility, arrivalism or boastfulness predominate. Such situations offer the possibility of comprehending one's own nature and vocation, of knowing oneself through confrontation with others.

consequence, with the universal creation. The work of art, therefore, is not a superficial or unconscious expression, the mere fruit of an instantaneous and fleeting 'inspiration' as happens in modern artistic representations, but an unrepeatable masterpiece. In this way participation with Tradition is determined, a full correspondence between the nature of man, his work and his authentic sacred end — an end which invests action, giving it a ritual character.

To a mechanistic and dehumanised vision of modern work is opposed the organic conception which the arts and trades had in the past; and to the contemporary worker, inserted into a standardised production line, is opposed the figure of the craftsman, who in his work seeks always a quality product, one of a kind. Two worlds, two styles, two realities opposed to one another: on the one hand material, quantity, uniformity and complacency, and on the other hand, the Sacred, quality, harmony and the beautiful.

Acknowledging the difficulties that nowadays can be entailed in determinate choices to 'return' to traditional craftsmanship and the cultivation of the earth as instruments for a dignified survival, the militant of the Tradition must keep clear regarding the meaning of the arts and the trades. While this kind of a life choice certainly requires attentive evaluation and does not represent a reckless flight from reality (the repercussions of which would be manifold, rendering many of the considerations made up to now vain), such a choice, at the same time, is not impossible and should not discouraged *a priori*. However much the present world is contaminated and adulterated in all its aspects, however much normality represents a distant utopia, craftsmanship and farming, if it is performed with the right attitude, yet conserve the distant germs of that impersonal action in which were founded the purity of honour and the dignity of a free being; they preserve the heritage of a working activity capable of being a rite, a symbol and a participation in Sacred Order.

8. YOUTH, BETWEEN ALIENATION AND MILITANCY

8.1 THE SOCIETY OF MEN

ADOLESCENCE IS the age of transition from the condition of infancy, when life passes in the midst of thoughtlessness and the protection of parents, to adulthood, when man must confront the necessities of his existence. It is the period of transition in which character takes shape, thanks to the familial upbringing one has received and experiences permitting comparison with the external world, which one begins to truly explore. The adolescent dedicates himself to his interests and his own personal sensibilities; he feels growing in him the sexual impulse and the necessity of a more complete life; he experiences the need for a greater independence and liberty; he manifests the tendency to want to destroy preconstituted schema and to swim against the current, continuously challenging common sense.

In Traditional civilisations, in which every epoch of a man's life was marked by specific ceremonies of a magico-religious character, the period of adolescence was accompanied by particular rites of passage from one existential condition to another. A special influence from on high was invoked, that this period should be 'assisted' by specific energies, such as could aid a profound transformation of being. This was an ontological change, in which the detachment from a simply sensible and physical existence introduced the youth to a new spiritual dimension, an alteration in state and a break in level which confirmed his entry into the world of the adults or the so-called 'society of men'. To this end, the overcoming of certain trials was the occasion to verify a youth's effective value and capacities. 'Special rites, called "rites of passage", often accompanied by a preliminary period of isolation of hard trials, aroused, according to a scheme of "death and rebirth", a new being, who alone could be considered a true man. Indeed, before this, the member of the group, whatever his age might be, was held to be a member of the women and the children, even of the animals themselves. Once he undergoes his transformation, the individual comes to pertain to the aggregate of the so-called "society of men". This society, having at once an initiatic (sacred) and warrior character, has power within the group. Its rights, like its responsibilities and its functions, are differentiated. It commands. It has a structure similar to that of an "Order".[1] Through such rites, the youth acquires the quality of a man, understood as *vir* (virility in the spiritual and active sense) and not as mere *homo* (virility in the naturalistic and passive sense), apprehending the values that constitute the basis of the 'society of men'; heroism, Honour, Fidelity, and the sacred vision at the foundation of existence. The gifts proper to youth, such as energy and enthusiasm, the capacity for unconditional devotion and intransigence, were valorised and ordered in such a way as to not be dispersed in a disordered and noisy exuberance.

From the historical point of view, one can find witness of these organisations in the feudal structures of the corporations and of the Knightly Orders, or also (as the legacy of these latter) in the constitution of student groups and associations during the development of the first Universities. To be participate in such groups and associations,

---

1   Julius Evola, 'Crisis of Modern Society', *Power and Hierarchy* (London: Arktos Media Ltd., publication forthcoming).

for example, it was necessary to possess particular virile gifts, to conform to a military style and to a special code of honour, to possess
a formation which did not disperse the moment one earned one's
academic title, but which lasted one's entire life, determining where
one belonged, marking one with a distinctive and qualifying sign even
when one worked a profession or held institutional offices. From such
associations, therefore, the future ruling class could be selected, and
youths directed toward the career which best suited them by their nature and character; the best could be rewarded and, at the same time,
those who were shown to be cowards and incompetents excluded.

8.2 THE FLIGHT FROM REALITY
AND LIFE AS 'NONSENSE'

Bourgeois and democratic levelling has atrophied the sacred and
heroic vision of the world, causing a rapid decline in the 'societies of
men' and the triumph of an individualistic, materialistic and hedonis-
tic worldview. The greatest consequences of this dissolutive process
are suffered precisely by the youngest generations who, deprived of
a higher point of reference, become the victims of a profound disorientation. Raised in the cult of comfort, where everything is permitted
and nothing must ever be lacking, in 'everything immediately' logic
typical of spoilt children, the educative model of contemporary society is the satisfaction of one's convenience, the dream of a career,
celebrity or wealth. Little does it matter if, in order to realise this
prospect, one must sacrifice things like one's conscience; what counts
is that one demands for oneself every kind of liberty which does not
run counter to the morality of 'minding one's own business'. This is
an absolute liberty that often transforms into the will to transgress,
into the desire to break through the sense of unease and anguish typical of those generations that come of age in a consumer society, and
which manifests itself in empty rebellion, in moral scepticism, in criti-
cism of every form of authority and in the favouring of an anarchical

and lawless life. This apparent anticonformism, in reality, becomes a ridiculous conformism, an adaptation to society and to its model, absorbed passively without any radical and effective reaction. Indeed, such forms of rebellion, rather than the reflection of a true need to break the schema, are nothing other than adrenaline shocks, equivalent to other experiences in which one makes an attempt to feel alive, to free oneself from one's rage in the face of the general indifference of this amorphous and boring world, to be noticed or to seem original in a society in which the aim is 'to have in life one's fifteen minutes of fame'.[2] However, one remains entrapped in the predefined schema that the system so ably provides, in those safety valves by which, it leads one to believe, one can change the world, when in reality one is merely enjoying one's last hour of air within the golden prison of contemporary society.[3] On the other hand, one has burnt one's vitality the previous evening in the disco or getting drunk at the pub, looking for collective entertainment, such as one can enjoy wholly within the group — that group which, in many cases, is the same 'band' or the 'tribe' which imbues one with the confidence to perpetrate actions one would never perform alone.

---

2   The expression is Andy Warhol's, a prominent figure in American pop-art, considered one of the most 'significant' personages of the 1900s on the artistic and creative plane.

3   Safety valves here are meant to refer to those experiences which are sociologically defined as 'deviant', which is to say, not in line with social conventions. For example, the phenomenon of 'hooliganism' fall into this category: through adequate media campaigns, the common man, the superficial man and the man lacking in the will to seek the 'Truth', as well as so-called 'hooligans', are led to believe that the incidents in the stadium represent a subversion of the social order and form the seed of a possible revolution. In reality, the system permits possibilities for release, as one grants to dogs in a park; that half an hour of apparent and absolute liberty notwithstanding, the leash is always ready and waiting for them. Thus, to the paradox posed by Ernst Jünger that it is 'better to be a delinquent than a bourgeois', one must respond in militant and revolutionary terms: 'neither delinquent *nor* bourgeois'.

The so-called escape in alcohol (drinking to forget), in drugs ("I can stop whenever I want"), in sex (pornography and unchecked vice), in the stadium or in the disco (violence and getting high) — all of this represents, therefore, extreme emotions that help one to forget a reality which is flat and deprived of colour;[4] these are the simplest and most immediate solutions to the need to stupefy oneself and think of nothing, to seek that euphoria that loosens the tension of existence.[5] Leaving one's right mind, distracting oneself and entertaining oneself continuously, feeling euphoria, abandoning oneself to a vortex of sensations, redefining oneself continually, giving oneself new forms through various and ever stronger emotions — thus does life become 'nonsense', bereft of certainty and full of disquiet.[6]

8.3 FRIENDSHIP AND CAMARADERIE: YOUTHS AMONG THE RUINS

In the individualistic and materialist society, human relations are often mutable and it is not easy to rediscover the value of true friendship, based as it is on a profound sentiment of affection beyond all convenience and utility. Today one light-heartedly confides the most

---

4   In Traditional civilisations, on the other hand, music, narcotics or inebriating drinks, carried a deeper meaning, insofar as they were considered as special applications of techniques aimed at reawakening in the person latent energies, toward the end of favouring their internal liberation.

5   It is interesting to note how youths, by their nature, have the habit of staying in company and living life cheerfully, showing vigour, enthusiasm and a certain dynamism. This peculiarity nowadays tends ever more to weaken in its positive side — which is to say, in the need to develop a spirit of community and camaraderie — while it tends to nourish the negative side — which is to say the incapacity to live in solitude without losing one's equilibrium. It suffices to consider the continual need for noise so as not to feel oneself alone, or the difficulty in concentration, in reading a book and reflecting, in thinking in solitude and experiencing it, not as an intolerable condition, but as an essential moment for finding oneself again.

6   Consider but the growing diffusion of so-called 'panic attacks'.

intimate secrets and confidences to 'untested' persons or persons one barely knows, and, overcoming all sense of shame, one grants them a license which end up causing misunderstandings, showing how the sense of distance and of the right relations between persons has been lost. Yet friendship is not merely collusion or role-playing, but is rather something deeper and truer which imbues a person's very way of being. In confirmation of this, we quote a passage from Cicero, where friendship is considered one of the gods of man, to such an extent that 'friendship can only exist between good men ... those whose actions and lives leave no question as to their honour, purity, equity, and liberality; who are free from greed, lust, and violence; and who have the courage of their convictions.' And again, 'In the face of a true friend a man sees as it were a second self. So that where his friend is he is; if his friend be rich, he is not poor; though he be weak, his friend's strength is his; and in his friend's life he enjoys a second life after his own is finished.'[7]

For the militant, his friends are comrades of that community with which he shares his daily battle; standing as they do in a normal relation founded on the Values of the Tradition, they cannot fail to be loyal, faithful and sincere. Camaraderie, like true friendship, is not founded on convenience, on insecurity or on weakness, but on reciprocal loyalty and respect, and it therefore appears natural to the militant to identify his friends as those who share his same experiences of growth and of struggle. It is normal to open oneself to a profound sense of love, and not simple confidence, with those who stand at one's side and, whatever benefits or material advantages should accrue to the relationship, it is right to emphasise that 'it is not friendship which confers advantage, but advantage which accompanies friendship'.

However, it should be clarified that, in principle, camaraderie is superior to friendship itself, or rather it encompasses it. The aims which lie at the basis of the relationship—the Idea (awareness

---

7   Cicero, *De Amicitia.*

through communal action), militancy (betterment following the formation and the rectification of character), style and ascesis, (clear, stable and coherent relations) — are all elements which elevate camaraderie. Between comrades, observations are made in an open and loyal spirit, with all necessary hardness, without offending one's fellow or descending with him into sterile arguments; among comrades, one accepts rebuke without rancour or resentment, and one resolves to make any effort rather than falling into the same error twice. Camaraderie is upheld by sincere confrontation, which defines the entire community of men who live in harmony, serenity, equilibrium, sharing a common feeling. To accept this confrontation means being willing to better oneself, bearing one's experiences to all the affairs that concern life, from political problems to organisational problems, from existential situations to questions of doctrine. This attitude is comprehensive and unresentful, because whatever is observed by one's comrade is aimed toward building and not destroying, helping and not offending, rectifying and not criticising.[8] However, opening up does not mean gossiping, since whatever is reported within the community belongs to the community;[9] camaraderie thus means neither adulation or servility, for if it were, it would no longer be an instrument for growth, but the premise for ruptures and discords. To confound it with complicity would be to substitute truth or loyalty with obsequiousness and deviousness, suspicions and misunderstandings, half words and half-truths; and above all it would be to substitute

---

8   Particular mention is reserved for whomever exercises the function of the leader or the authority within the group. His words, his observations, his rebukes, etc., must have the nature of an act of love with respect to the militant, a measured and direct gesture for a person who is hierarchically different from him, but who is his equal in terms of dignity. For this reason it is said that the leader is he who 'serves' and not he who is 'served'.

9   Indeed, it would be profoundly wrong to take up fail to make observations, since this absence could be the evident sign of a lack of love and of attention for oneself, for the comrade one has in front of one and for the entire community as a whole.

hierarchy with hierarchism, which is to say the parody of a pseudo-authority lacking in legitimacy, where individualism and the absence of virtue rule.

Camaraderie and militancy, therefore, are complementary, because the latter unites, cements and determines one's belonging. The comrade is a comprehending and loveable brother; before asking favours he is ready to give aid, and he does not look for banal excuses to see to his convenience, nor puts his comrades into stupid difficulties. This is an opening in love which requires a response in love: one seeks nothing in return, for camaraderie is a total and disinterested giving of oneself; camaraderie is brotherhood before the spirit.

On this subject, Léon Degrelle says, 'We will escape from this decadence only through an immense moral rectification, by teaching men to love, to sacrifice themselves, to live, to fight and to die for a higher ideal. In an age in which one lives only for oneself, it will be necessary for hundreds, thousands of men to live, no longer for themselves, but for a common ideal: they must be ready from the very beginning for any sacrifice for this ideal, for any humiliation, any act of heroism. What counts are faith and faithfulness, the total absence of egoism and individualism, the tension of one's whole being toward "service" — however thankless this service might be, and wherever it must be carried out — service to a cause that goes beyond man, which demands everything of him, without promising him anything in return. What counts are the qualities of soul, its vibrations, total dedication, the will to hold an ideal high above everything else, and to do so in the spirit of the most absolute disinterestedness. When the hour comes to save the world, there will be need of a handful of heroes and saints to carry out the Reconquista.'

9. THE REVOLT AGAINST THE WORLD OF THE MASSES

9.1 CONTEMPORARY POLITICS AND THE NEW WORLD ORDER

IN THE COURSE of the last century, up until our own days, contemporary politics has ever more taken on the features of a theatrical representation composed of directors, actors, dwarves, ballerinas, puppets and puppetmasters. Care for the 'common weal', on the local level, has translated into the exaltation of personalistic and plebeian interests within a system of malfeasance and of ethical and moral decadence; and on the national level, in the affirmation of a State which is an empty container, the executor of decisional processes which are all decided elsewhere, in a manner which has almost nothing about it of transparency and 'democracy'.

However much literature and cinema has been produced on the theme of the 'great universal conspiracy', not to speak of disinformation and even science fiction, the thesis of the New World Order is extremely current and is supported by events and phenomena which, in the course of history, have followed one upon another up to our own days; by now it is a well-known fact that, beyond mere appearances, there really exist centres of 'occult power' which are capable of determining events and manipulating public opinion. Examples of international meetings on the part of clubs and secret societies behind closed doors, in which participation is strictly reserved to politicians, economists, Masons, representatives of the great multinational corporations, bankers, etc., are nowadays easily verifiable even through the news. And why do these men gather together, what is their goal? The phenomenon would clearly merit a more thorough study, but here we limit ourselves to indicating some of its principal characteristics.

The progressivist idea of a new world and of a renovated humanity has always accompanied Protestantism, especially Anglo-Saxon Protestantism, and has reinforced itself over the course of the centuries thanks to the contribution of Masonic universalism and neo-messianism. The revolutions which followed, in particular the French Revolution but also all the revolutions which characterised the advent of the national states in the nineteenth century, have always borne the common stamp of bringing an attack on the traditional world, which, however fallen and decadent it may have been, was still permeated with a vision of the world founded on the Sacred. The peculiarity of these revolutions, apart from what is taught in the official history books, is that they were never spontaneous, but were prompted and guided by elites and occult societies capable of directing from behind the scenes. In this regard, let us recall that Julius Evola dedicates an important chapter to the so-called occult war, just as we find a very interesting study of it in the work of Emmanuel Malynksi.[1]

---

1   Cf. J. Evola, *Men Among the Ruins*; *Il genio d'Israele*, Edizioni Il Cinabro, Catania 1992; *Fenomenologia della Sovversione*, edizioni SeaR, Borzano 1993; *Scritti sulla Massoneria*, Edizioni Arya, Genova 2012. Cf. E. Malynski, *The Occult War* (Logik, 2016); *Fedeltà feudale e dignità umana*, Edizioni Ar, Padova 2014; *Il Proletarismo*, Edizioni Ar, Padova 1979. We make note also of Maurizio Blondet, *Cronache dell'Anticristo*, Edizioni Effedieffe, Proceno 2011; *Adelphi della dissoluzione*, Edizioni Effedieffe, Proceno 2013; *Tutti i complotti*, Edizioni Effedieffe, Proceno 2013; *Chi comanda in America*, Edizioni Effedieffe, Milan 2004; *Israele, Usa, il terrorismo islamico*, Edizioni Effedieffe, Milan 2005. See also E. Perucchetti and G. Marletta, *Governo Globale*, Edizioni Arianna, Bologna 2013; *La Fabbrica della manipolazione*, Edizioni Arianna, Bologna 2014. [The works listed in Italian have yet to be translated into English. — Trans.]

Today, with the possibility offered by modern instruments of mass communication, not just the television but also the internet and all of its 'social' derivatives, the opportunity to direct these phenomena has become yet more tempting, and to do so moreover without relying on necessarily violent forms: the manipulation of information and the creation of a specifically oriented public opinion is the most insidious and effective means of affirming a new dominant system, such as is capable of penetrating our consciousness and directing our behaviour. However, a certain kind of nature always re-emerges, inherent as it is in the egalitarian coercion proper to the democratic system — which, notwithstanding its façade of bleeding-heart pacifism, has brought about forms of conflict 'in all those human and social relations which normally would stand in a relation of organic complementarity', generating conditions of hostility between individual and State, employee and employer, man and woman, etc., and a crisis among communitarian organisations.[2]

Exploiting this situation, therefore, the New World Order, or rather those who promote it, have had an easy time of it in our days; for today the sensation of existing within an enormous controlled and controlling network is more than cinematographic fantasy, but is rather the sad reality perceived even by the most unconscious among us. To summarise what the New World Order is — or what it will be — we recall a phrase by an illustrious representative of the banking lobby, David Rockefeller, which he uttered in June of 1991,

---

2   See G. Alì, 'Democrazia e violenza', in *Heliodromos* n. 19, 21 April 2008, and also G. Alì, *Indirizzi per l'azione tradizionale. Scritti di educazione e formazione militante* (Rome: Raido, 2013). The Tradition, which does not conceive of democracy, considers the State to be an organic unity in the spiritual sense as well as the naturalistic sense: a hierarchical unity subject to a superior principle of political sovereignty (spiritual and political: *Imperium*), which unites people to one and the same principle and one and the same law, in which the parts are united by a bond of solidarity without any particular one of them or any particular faction prevailing over the others: there exist no divisions, individualisms or sectarianisms.

during the Baden-Baden "Bilderberg" meeting: 'But the world is now more sophisticated and is prepared to march toward a world government. ... The supranational sovereignty of an intellectual elite and world bankers is surely preferable to the national auto-determination that was practised in past centuries.' This would be a government whose aspiration, therefore, is to create a unique centre of transnational power controlled by an elite, through the affirmation of an officially approved single thought such as would destroy every kind of identity (be it political, religious, sexual, etc.), and lead to the triumph of Subversion and of the so-called reign of Satan.

Leaving aside the political side of this question in its widest meaning, let a final consideration be conceded us in the teeth of those who today represent the elect of the people — which is to say, the exponents of democracy, they who today decide our lives. As Alexis Carrel observes, 'the democratic principle has contributed to the weakening of civilisation, impeding the development of the best, while it is evident that individual inequalities ought to be respected. There are, in modern society, functions appropriate to the great, to the little, to the middling, and to the inferior; but one must not expect to form superior individuals with the same procedures which are valid for the weak. The standardisation of the human creatures on the part of the democratic ideal has assured the predominance of the mediocre. They are everywhere preferred to the strong: they are aided, protected, often admired. ... Since it was impossible to lift up the inferior, the only means to produce equality amongst men was to bring them all to a lower level: in this way, the force of personality disappears.'[3] It is evident how the disappearance of the aristocracy of the spirit, in favour of the violent emergence of the plebs, has brought about a gradual social and political malaise, a vulgarisation and a decadence in values which the *Vishu-Purana* describes in this way, in a what is, to say the least, a prophetic manner:

---

3   In *Heliodromos*, new series, n. 19.

Races of servants, of outcasts, and of barbarians will make themselves the masters of the shores of the Indus, of the Darvika, of the Chandrabhaga and of the Kashmir. ... The rulers of the world, as violent natures ... will rule it over all goods and over their subjects. Limited in their power, the many will rapidly rise and rapidly fall. Brief will be their lives, insatiable their desires, and they will know almost nothing of piety. The peoples of various countries, intermixing with them, will follow their example. The prevalent caste will be that of the servants. They who possess will desert agriculture and commerce and will make their living as servants or in mechanical professions. The rulers, rather than protecting their subjects, will despoil them and under fiscal pretexts will steal the properties of the merchant caste. Sanity and law will diminish day by day until the world will be completely perverted. Possessions alone will confer rank. The single motive for devotion will be the concern for physical health, the only connection between the genders will be pleasure, the only path to attain success in any competition will be fraud. The earth will be venerated for its mineral treasures alone. Priestly garments will substitute the dignity of the priest. Weakness will be the only reason for obedience. The race will be incapable of producing divine births. Deviated by unbelievers, men will insolently ask, "What authority have the traditional texts? What are these Gods, what is the caste which holds spiritual authority?" Respect for the castes, for the social order and for the [traditional] institutions will fail in the dark age. Marriages in this age will cease to be a rite and the laws connecting a disciple to a spiritual Master will no longer have any strength. It will be thought that anyone can arrive by any path at the state of regeneration, and the acts of devotion which can still be performed will no longer produce any result.

Every order of life will be equal for all. Those who distribute the greatest amounts of money will be the lords of men, and familial descent will cease to be a title of pre-eminence. Men will focus all their interests on the acquisition, even the dishonest acquisition, of riches.

Every species of man will believe himself to be equal to a Brahmin. The people will have more terror than ever of death and will fear penury: for this reason alone they will have the form of a cult. Women shall follow the will neither of husbands nor of parents. They will be egoists, despicable, decentred and mendacious, and will attach themselves to the dissolute. They will become simple objects of sexual disintegration. Impiety will prevail among these men, deviated by heresy.[4]

9.2 BEYOND AN ANACHRONISTIC VISION

Beginning in the post-war period, the world of the 'right' has seen parties, movements and mottos following one after another; all of them have claimed, in their vision of the world, an indissoluble connection with Fascism. Beyond the real or presumed convictions of those who play a part in all of this, many of whom have been successively integrated into the system, it is needful to note the error in every anachronistic vision bound to history, such as are often the fruit of a doctrinaire kind of confusion.[5] Indeed, the fascination with and respect for Fascism cannot emerge from the basis of elements and phenomena connected to specific historical contexts, which are inevitably connected to men and to facts which by now have passed, but rather insofar as the fascist movements of the twentieth century

---

4　The 'Purana' are texts of cosmological character, whose purpose was the religious education of those who did not pertain to the *dvija* (the first three castes), which is to say, of the *sudra*, women and the casteless. The text here has been taken from J. Evola in the appendix of *Revolt Against the Modern World*. In the *Bhagavata Purana*, too, it is written: 'The law of the heretics will prevail, rulers will act as brigands; men will give themselves to theft, to lies, to useless delights, to every kind of shameless action. … When deceit, mendacity, confusion, turbulence, and sadness rules, we are in the Age of Iron. … During this period men are greedy, lawless, ruthless, gratuitously hostile, miserable, gluttonous, … women libertine and base, … peoples exploited by kings. … Individuals who do not know anything other than injustice administer justice by seating themselves in the highest places. … Enough that one is poor, to be bad; hypocritical, to be good; living together, to be married. The supreme goal of all will be to fill their bellies. … The castes will all be like to that of the *shudra*.'

5　We should also note the case of those who claim Jacobin, Risorgimental, liberal, Masonic, vaguely patriotic and nationalistic visions and methodologies, all of which, rather than undermining the democratic system (whose genesis is in point of fact Jacobin, Risorgimental, liberal, Masonic, and nationalistic), reinforce it.

sought, with all their limitations, to politically affirm the Principles of the Tradition. The force of these movements and, at the same time, their capacity to be truly revolutionary, have their origins in Spiritual Principles such as Honour, Loyalty, Fidelity, and Sacrifice, which once made them effectively great. Thus, it is not so much a question of the right social formulae, however valid and timely they may be, but rather of the right style; which is as much as to say that man and his formation according to Traditional Principles must precede it. On the other hand, it was already clear to those men who gave life to the revolutions of the twentieth century that the essence of political doctrine and action was not to be found in political programmes, but had to be sought in the Spiritual Principle that characterised the fascist revolutions as against those that were animated by false liberal and Marxist premises.

It follows from this that, for the militant, political action has a sense and plays its noble role, supposing only that it is sustained by a spiritual vision of life, without which there can be no solidarity, no Fatherland, no people. 'We see our true fatherland in the *Idea*. Not to all be of one and the same land or of one and the same language, but to all be of one and the same idea, that is what counts today. ... To the collectivistic unity of the nation — *des enfants de la patrie* — which has ever more predominated since the Jacobin revolution, we in any case oppose something: namely, an Order, men faithful to a principle, witnesses of a higher authority and legitimacy proceeding precisely from the Idea'.[6]

The ties binding us to a world which is destined to fade must be cut with extreme realism; we must not linger on attempts to exhume the past, but seek rather to affirm and concretise the ideas of the Tradition, the only universal and eternal ideas there are. Having abandoned the disorderly and approximate forms and the confused appeals to a sense of honour and fidelity, today one must carry out

---

6   J. Evola, *Orientamenti*, Point 8.

a serious work of witness which renders the Values of the spirit and of the Tradition visible, that they might become absolute measures and affirmations. This witness, on the basis of the qualifications of the militant and on objective conditions, can manifest in any field, even in the political if there is need. Apropos of this, it is indeed not contrary to revolutionary logic to conceive of the militant's participation within the present political system, should only he be qualified, well-oriented and sufficiently 'armoured', and so long as his function is exclusively consecrated to the cause — which is to say, that he be an 'instrument' for advancing battles or for intervening for the Idea, in a such a way as to realistically facilitate it. But he must remain different from that system in his style, must not permit himself to be contaminated in his depths, must not end up like those who, in order to battle the system from within it, become its principal defenders (with all attendant perks...).

9.3 THE LAW OF ELECTIVE AFFINITIES

'Like awakens like, like attracts like, like joins again to like.'[7] The law of elective affinities demonstrates how far the Traditional point of view lies from empty electoral slogans and from all democratic whimsy for proselytising; rather than wasting time in convincing anyone, the militant must concern himself with his style of life, thereby becoming an example and raising the awareness, through deeds and not words, of whomever is internally prepared to accept the Traditional path. To dwell on the hope of convincing those who have neither the interest nor still less the will to conform their existence to Tradition is so much wasted effort and loss of time: for two different essences and human substances cannot unite with one another.

To whomever keeps his eyes essentially on quality, therefore, the quantitative question is absolutely secondary, given that it is not the

---

7   J. Evola, *Men Among the Ruins*, Chapter 5, 'Bonapartism — Machiavellianism — Elitism'.

number of votes or the number of members to form a group which determine its strength, but rather the existence within it of formed, rectified and qualified men. Duration in time and the power to leave a sign, past all the personages that will follow, is that kind of qualitative reflection which the community, even if it be scarce in numbers, must always make reference.

The law of elective affinities, therefore, empowers the militant, who takes as his own the motto 'less preaching and more example'. However, this kind of radicalism must never translate into the erroneously rigid attitude of him who is ready to pass his judgements and to declaim the doctrine as though it were a catechism. This 'crustacean-like' nature, by which a man tends to put up a hard front in an exclusively exterior form, so as to mask an inner fragility and softness, is one of the risks which the militant, especially at the beginning of his path, soon faces. Many are the cases of those who, in their resolve to cast judgement on the problems of others, use this as a suspect justification for their own weaknesses, and many are the examples of those who, having followed this path, and in view of the possibility of landing a career or putting up a family, have put their good intentions in the drawer. One must never lose a certain necessary elasticity in facing the trials that this world puts to us; we must be as those reeds which bend but do not break before the tempest, and which are always ready to regain their original upright position.

Being conscious that the crisis of society is the reflection of the crisis of man, it is indispensable to exert oneself in stirring new forms of sensibility, through the formation of new men who know how to be worthy witnesses to the Tradition through their example.

9.4 AN OPERATIONAL METHOD: THE THREE PLANES

From an operational point of view, and recapitulating what we have so far explained within this book, we may for simplicity's sake say that the attention of the militant must concentrate on three different planes, all closely connected. Presupposing that the action (the reflex of consciousness) is the touchstone for judging a man and his work, the three planes are the worldly plane of comparison and improvement, within which the militant proves himself, day after day, with the goal of rediscovering his own centre. The first plane is the existential plane: social relations, sex and love, the family, study and work, every situation or affair of daily life are tests to measure oneself, spheres in which it is important to behave with coherency, loyalty and respect, keeping faith with one's word, being correct and clear with everyone. It is the field in which one might verify one's interior bearing and one's proper level of qualification with respect to the Principles of the traditional order.

The second plane is the communitarian.[8] While the militant is alone in his choices and in his evaluations, and knows that the one and definitive response to the trials of life must come from his life, at the same time he is not alone in the struggle for the Tradition, and he knows that there is a community which will aid and sustain him; there are men, like him, determined to better themselves, ready to offer their shield in battle, to protect their comrade in his difficulties. The Community is an indispensable aid to educate the militant to constancy and to the unconditional dedication for an Idea, to disinterested sacrifice, to responsibility and to the assumption of tasks

---

8   See *A Handbook of Traditional Living*, Part Two: The Front of Tradition, Chapter 12, 'The Operative Unit' (London: Arktos Media Ltd., 2010), in which broad indications are given for the organisation and the development of an organic community.

which must be performed with the greatest care and with the force of one's initiative.[9]

Finally, there is the spiritual plane, the most important, being as it is the prerequisite to lucid, conscious and oriented action. The militant, in an intimate and personal interior dialogue, meditates on those actions which he has done and which he has yet to do, analyses the negative aspects of his character, reflects in silence on the meaning of his path. In the face of the whirlwind of contemporary life, of the frenetic agitation of daily living, he pauses to rediscover his calm and his interior tranquillity. And he accomplishes this work through indispensable doctrinal support, through study and educational texts and texts of traditional knowledge that, supported by correct action, permit the militant to assimilate their contents, leading to a consequent and tangible rectification of his style: it is not his head which fills up with notions, but his heart which fills with truth.

The above is a simplification of an operational method which transposes, on the plane of the militant, the traditional tripartition of the human being into body, soul and spirit. The path to reconquer oneself and the affirmation of new men depend on the application of each of these, with sacrifice and diligence, and on the constant quest for equilibrium.[10]

---

9   It is to be hoped that every community gives life to economic activity, wherein its own militants can work, thus offering to those who have need of such a dignified occupation, and at the same time directing the youngest militants toward work experience. Cf. also *Quaderni di Kulturkampf*, 'La comunità militante', edited by Raido, on www.raido.it and www.azionetradizionale.com.

10 For the analogy between the tripartition body-soul-spirit and the red-white-black colours of the flag of the Tradition, see *Quaderni di Kulturkampf*, 'Il rosso, il bianco, il nero. La bandiera della Tradizione', edited by Raido, on www.raido.it and www.azionetradizionale.com.

10. SPIRIT AND RELIGIOSITY[1]

10.1 RELIGIONS AND CHRISTIANITY

THE TERM 'RELIGION', whose etymological meaning is 'that which rejoins', 'that which binds' man with the Sacred, presupposes that at a certain past moment participation with the divine became no longer spontaneous and natural. There came a distancing from the Centre, symbolically represented as a 'fall', which has led to the birth of various traditions and particular religions — which is to say, centres which are secondary with regard to the Primordial Tradition from which all of them derive. Such a multiplicity of traditional paths is necessary on account of the different nature of various peoples, insofar as each leads back to a unique Truth, confirming, in its symbols and in its rituals, the *transcendent unity of the religions.* Thus, the spiritual influence transmitted by each religion has a single origin and a single fount, and religion, as Guénon underlines, lies in the order of eternal truths concerning the first origins and the final ends. Moreover, religion transmits those rules of life that must be respected if man is to establish a relation with the divine and break free of the material conditionings that constrain him.

---

1 The theme here in consideration has already been tackled in its doctrinal aspects in the first and second books for the formation of the militant of the Tradition. Within the present study we limit ourselves to providing certain useful indications for an existential approach to the question.

Unfortunately, in the course of the ages and in particular following the affirmation of the modern world and the advent of the last times, the religions, just as the other Traditional institutions, have suffered from a process of decadence and obfuscation, remaining all the while the best instrument for participating in the Universal Principle. A process of decadence came, characterised by the progressive human-isation and individualisation of the Sacred, and reducing ever more to a mostly sentimental, emotive and mental factor. This is very evident in the case of Christianity, which is to say, the principal religion of the Western world, for the form it has taken is that of a vague religiosity and a morality, a mere sentimental affair which prevails over doctrine and over the intellectual order.[2]

However, it is important to clarify that even when religion is taken as a simple moral model to adhere to so as to distinguish be-tween 'good' and 'evil', it remains ever a brake to the appetites and to the *ego*, and participation in a religious practice, though it be merely the fruit of habit, and thus not wholly conscious, can remain a last defence which, in moments of profound crisis like the present, might favour a climate suitable for the grafting of forces from on high.[3] In contemporary Western society, which is by now secularised and

---

2   In the West, religion is manifested as the union between three elements. The highest is *dogma*, which represents the intellectual and transcendent part unit-ing man to the divine. The second is *morality*, which represents the social part, in which the sentimental elemental has a primary role and which manifests as *belief*. The third element is given by the *cult* and more precisely by the ritual element that participates both in the dogmatic-intellectual element, and the moral-sentimental element. The rites have an intellectual character insofar as they are the symbolic and sensible expression of doctrine, but they also have a social character insofar as they are practices that require the participation of the faithful. So soon as the elemental sentimental prevails over the intellectual, the religion declines into moralism. See R. Guénon, *Introduction to the Study of the Hindu Doctrines* (Sophia Perennis, 2004).

3   Consider in this context the influence exercised by the sacraments that at least 'virtually' are capable of calling down 'grace' — a force from on high — which is capable of vivifying and sanctifying.

desacrilised, the observation of Christian precepts, for instance, is for many an instrument of 'salvation', so as to receive a moral, 'legislative', 'ritual' and dogmatic support, guaranteeing, at the same time, a connection with the divine world, however much it might be on the whole devotional and sentimental.[4] Over the course of the ages, even up to our days, in which the attacks on Christianity have been ever more and ever more frequent,[5] the process of degeneration has not spared the Catholic Church itself, within which 'the smokes of Satan' seem to have penetrated in a flagrant manner. Beginning above all in the last century, as some have justly noted, Christianity perished of fright before the world, a world that wants it 'wan and weakly, anxious to obtain a right to citizenship in a society which despises it'.[6] And one is left 'perplexed' by certain positions taken by the ecclesiastical hierarchy in support of the New World Order, as exemplified by a series of comments made by Pontiffs such as Paul VI, John Paul II and Benedict XVI on official occasions, thus confirming that the globalist lobby is powerfully rooted even in the Church.[7] As Guénon observes,

---

4   Within Christianity two substantially contrary tendencies can be distinguished: the one which shows traces of the sentimental aspect, wherein fear of God predominates, along with charity, hope, humility, a mysticism which is the abandonment and the crumbling of the soul, a morality attentive more to mortification than to a true ascesis. The other tendency brings Christianity back to the Universal idea, and it is to it that one must refer to grasp its traditional Aryan-Romano, solar, heroic and aristocratic essence. With the prevalence of one tendency over the other, the compassionate-Mediterranean or the warrior-Roman, one can comprehend the various and sometimes contrary positions that Christianity has taken over the course of its history.

5   Consider the day at hand and the 'crusades' in favour of the new rights recognised by contemporary society: abortion, genetic manipulations, homosexuality, ethical relativism, etc., are but a few examples of the attacks brought against the Catholic Church.

6   E. Perucchetti and G. Marletta, *La fabbrica della manipolazione*, Arianna editrice, Bologna 2014, p. 155.

7   John Paul II, in his homily of 1 January, 2004, asserted: 'People are becoming more and more aware of the need for *a new international order*'. Benedict XVI,

Catholicism has been 'struck by the tendencies of the modern spirit — not in its principle, but in the way in which it is usually presented: under the pretext of rendering it acceptable to the current mentality, ever more untoward concessions are made, and in this way one encourages that which one should rather energetically fight against'.[8]

Surely, it should be recalled how the Second Vatican Council (1962) played a blatant role in this; during that Council, the Church decided to abandon its mission as interpreter of the Tradition, preferring to give pre-eminence to its sociological, humanitarian and moralistic aspect. At the same time, it should be specified that a certain perplexity is to be found even in the so-called 'traditionalist Catholic' circles, whose often sectarian exclusivism is harbinger of an adversarial and polemical attitude and (what is unfortunately all too frequent) of attacks on the Traditional doctrine itself and its foremost interpreters, such as Guénon and Evola, who are accused improperly of being the instruments of subversion and of 'demonry'. Such cliquish attacks, as happens often, end up promoting Subversion rather than combatting it, as is witnessed by the latest in a long list of failures to comprehend the message of the Tradition as standing beyond the signs of the times.

---

on December 25, 2005, stated in his *Urbi et Orbi* message: 'Men and women of today, humanity come of age yet often still so frail in mind and will, let the Child of Bethlehem take you by the hand! Do not fear; put your trust in him! The life-giving power of his light is an incentive for building a new world order based on just ethical and economic relationships.'

8   Guénon also adds: 'Let us not insist on the blindness of those who, under the pretext of "tolerance", make themselves unconscious accomplices of real counterfeits to religion, whose hidden intent they are far from suspecting. We only mention in passing, in this regard, the deplorable abuse that is frequently made of the word "religion" itself: do we not hear every moment the use of expressions like "religion of the fatherland", "religion of science", "religion of duty"? This is not simple linguistic negligence, it is symptom of the confusion that reigns everywhere in the modern world, since language at bottom does nothing but faithfully represent the state of souls; and such expressions are incompatible with the true religious sense'. Cf. R. Guénon, *Symbols of the Sacred Science* (Sophia Perennis, 2004).

10.2 NEOSPIRITUALISM[9]

The climate of profound mistrust and confusion created by Subversion, not to speak of the process of the secularisation of religion, has brought many to seek safe harbour in a whole galaxy of sects and 'religious movements', which are devoid of any spiritual principle. Not by accident has Subversion on the one hand declared war on the legitimate religions, destroying the ancient traditions, while on the other hand offered straight up surrogates for spirituality which are decidedly more compatible with the feeling of the 'new world' — mere parodies of religion whose aim is to 'neutralise' even those who really feel a sincere need for spirituality.

Thus legitimate religion is substituted with a new religion — neospiritualism — which crushes the previous spiritual founts and leaves man at the mercy of diabolic forces. Contemporary society is a pullulation of movements fascinated by esotericism, by oriental religions, by occultism, by spiritism, by extraterrestrials, by magic, by secret societies and by every kind of mysticism, the result of all of this being nothing other than a dangerous syncretism, which can go so far as to produce a kind of religious hybridisation. A rather well-known example of this is the 'New Age' movement, which arose in the last decades of the last century. It is a kind of neospiritualist cauldron lacking in any kind of definitive doctrine, fit for everyone and for every taste. This new spirituality, affirmed everywhere today, is a perfect example of the modern spirit and is absolutely consistent with the 'new world'; it is intolerant of every legitimate rule, is devoid of personality and identity and therefore, in point of fact, represents a disintegrating element for traditional identities. It is the bringer of a new relation with the Sacred constructed in the image and semblance of man, inspired

---

9   On neospiritualism, J. Evola has published some important works, including *Maschera e volto dello spiritualismo contemporaneo* (Rome: Edizioni Mediterranee, 2008). See also R. Guénon, *The Reign of Quantity and the Signs of the Times* (Sophia Perennis, 2001).

by absolute individualism. Amongst the most widespread and fashionable beliefs, we recall the theory of 'reincarnation', sustained by the better part of neospiritualist movements, with the Theosophical Society and the Anthroposophical Society at their head, which bears witness to the confusion persisting between the psychic and the spiritual elements.[10]

This last is one of the most dangerous characteristics of that neospiritualism which stands at the bottom, in particular, of various forms of occultism (Masonry, spiritism, Satanism, summoning practices, ceremonial magic, etc.), through which an opening is produced to the subterranean states of the human psyche, causing a 'dangerous breakdown' of the protective wall that defends man from the nefarious influences of dark forces.[11] Spiritual research, confused as it is and deprived of doctrinal foundations, transforms into the cultivation of 'powers', through, for example, evocative and divinatory practices, leaving the individual the prisoner of his own suggestion and exposed to every kind of abandonment and interior slackening. The end result is that this emphasis on the emotive and interest in the sensational comes to alter consciousness itself; there comes an opening to subterranean states of the human psyche, which is to say, of the seat of the subconscious which, insofar as it is a state of psychic obfuscation in

---

10   Many, incorrectly interpreting the *law of karma*, hold that reincarnation is the basis of the idea of individual evolution that a being accomplishes in order to liberate himself from his individualism. In reality it is a question of the latest confusion on the different possibilities of the afterlife, which is to say, the road toward Liberation and salvation, the phenomena of transmigration and of metempsychosis, the reabsorption of the individual faculties, the walk upon the road of the gods or of the Fathers, etc. For a good study of these things, we will mention the works of René Guénon *Man and His Becoming According to the Vedanta* (Sophia Perennis, 2001), as well as Julius Evola, *Maschera e volto dello spiritualismo contemporaneo*.

11   Among the characteristics of neospiritualism it is easy to recognize a mixture of modern ideas like universal brotherhood (egalitarianism and democracy), progress (evolution and scientism), naturalism (vegetarianism and animalism), pacifism, feminism, etc.

which the impressions and the conditionings of the external world are stored, becomes the object of influences of the worst kind.[12] The subconscious is the shadow cone of man, and indeed represents the preferred field of action of Subversion, which, in its operation of manipulating the consciousness, intervenes by continuously arousing fears, desires, agitations, illusions, disturbances, disequilibriums and instabilities; and these, insinuating themselves into the individual, lead to unhappy and conditioned states.

Therefore, the work of formation and rectification of character is indispensable for the militant toward the end of acquiring an ever greater consciousness and vigilance over himself, so that these 'pseudo-ideas' will contaminate him as little as possible, and, at the same time, so that they will be as much as possible circumscribed and destroyed. The study of the causes and the effects at the basis of neo-spiritualist 'tumours' is the prerequisite for that work of truth which the militant must carry through, by unmasking and countering the subtlest forms that would deviously deviate him from his path and would favour the subversive project, aiming at devastation and the 'overturning' everything which is normal and legitimate.[13]

---

12 What is recorded by the subconscious might re-emerge involuntarily and without being recalled or desired; consider, for example, an image seen in the past or during a moment of distraction, which re-emerges unexpectedly, just as unusual attitudes or aspects of the character which manifest spontaneously.

13 Among the characteristics of these diabolic manifestations we can list the writing, reciting, representing symbols, rites, formulae, prayers, and normal sacraments backwards, up to the stupidest and most unconscious manipulations.

10.3 NEOPAGANISM[14]

Many, in their need for spirituality, respond by seeking fulfilment in the pagan religions of the past — Egyptian, Roman, Celtic or Germanic — in all their respective and numerous nuances. Fascinated and mesmerised by a world of gods, rites, myths and symbols, these, through an operation that leaves a great deal to the imagination, attempt to awaken ancient forces which have long been slumbering, thereby 'historicising' the Sacred and disregarding the one and eternal Universal Principle, which, from time to time, adopts the most suitable forms for the times and places in which man lives. When a Traditional form degenerates, which is to say when its spiritual essence retires, becoming inaccessible to the common man, only the vestiges and the ruins remain to bear witness to a past action, in much the same way as those 'psychic residues' which continue to wander in the 'larval' state after the death of a human being. Whenever a tradition withdraws, without leaving any continuity in its transmission, the places, the objects and its exterior forms can become the prey of the emissaries of Counter-tradition, which is to say of him who is called, in the various traditions, the 'Adversary', the 'Ape of God', the 'False Prophet', the 'Deceiver' or the 'Antichrist'. It is no accident that Satanic gatherings take place in proximity to ruins, deconsecrated churches, cemeteries, and structures that once served as the support for spiritual realities and which are today abandoned, giving life to an authentic cult of the dead. For this reason, a Latin saying has it that *corruptio*

---

14 On neopaganism, we note the writings of J. Evola and R. Guénon. See the fundamental argument by J. Evola, 'L'equivoco del neo-paganesimo', in *Bibliografia Fascista*, February 1936 and *Maschera e volto dello spiritualismo contemporaneo*, cit. See also the first two chapters of Guénon's *Symbols of Sacred Science* (Sophia Perennis, 2004), and Chapters 26 and 27 of *The Reign of Quantity and the Signs of the Times* (Sophia Perennis, 2001).

optimi pessima, meaning that 'that which was best, once it has been corrupted, is the worst'.[15]

In the framework of the cyclical vision, which is a pilaster of the Traditional doctrine, paganism is nothing other than an intermediate stage, prior to the very disorder that still today continues its dissolutive process. The Tradition is not that of museums, of art monuments and literature, nor is it a religion of the dead, of the archaeologists or the historians of religion. The Tradition is above all style, character, formation, ascesis and discipline, and, as Julius Evola underlines, 'the elements of Style have an evidence all their own; they are not tied to times passed; they can act in any given period as formative forces for the character and can hold as ideals, so soon as a corresponding vocation awakens. *They have a normative value. In the worst of cases, they have the value of a measure*'.[16] For this reason, to think that the pagan religion is preferable to the Catholic religion means to fail to understand how paganism has nothing living about it, and still less can

---

15   After the death of a man, for periods of varying lengths, psychic residues remain, or rather forces that belong to a 'subtle state', the intermediate world of the soul; this, in contrast to the body, which is destined to decompose, and the spirit, which is destined for other 'states', leaves traces as if they were continuations of what came before. These are the object and the instrument for the perpetuation of dark forms, insofar as psychic residues are 'errant influences', forces which are neither material nor spiritual, which conserve only the illusory appearance of a being. The spiritual influences, in order to act have need of a basis both of psychic (subtle) order and corporeal (gross-material) order, represented by objects and/or by men. When spiritual influences withdraw, the bases remain charged with these same psychic forces which will be as strong and persistent as the spiritual element which used them was powerful. The bases (ruins, cadavers, etc.), once they have been deprived of the spiritual element and reduced to a larval state, are easy prey for the dark forces of the Counter-Tradition. This is the deepest and most delicate aspect, and at the same time the least explored and least known aspect, of what is called the Occult War. Cf. J. Evola, *Maschera e volto dello spiritualismo contemporaneo*, and *The Reign of Quantity and the Signs of the Times* (Sophia Perennis, 2001).

16   J. Evola, *Men Among the Ruins*, Chapter 14, 'Latin Character — Roman World — Mediterranean Soul', part two.

boast any legitimate continuity. Indeed, to fill the many lacunae of the doctrine that one wishes to exhume, one often has to take recourse to additions which are the fruit of personal inventions or interpretations (subjectivism) — all the more evidence of the limits of the operation of reconstructing the continuity and the 'uninterrupted chain' of the pagan tradition, wherein exponents of occultism and Masonry often pop up. These are today deviant and anti-Traditional realities, when they are not 'counter-initiating'.[17]

While in the case of the youngest, one can suppose that such errors are carried out in good faith, in other cases, the 'masters of the situation' cannot and should not have any justification, since there are a multitude of pernicious consequences of any choice wed to genuine subversive practices. The same anti-Catholic obsession of the neopagans appears equally suspect since, as has already been observed in the case of the polemical and adversarial attitude of Catholic traditionalists, the attack on a traditional form does nothing other than favour the anti-Traditional front.

Rather than dwelling on an attempt to prop up constructions which were once magnificent but today today dilapidated and in ruins, the man of the Tradition must look on upward and not backward, since turning to the past means wishing to drink of stagnant water, when one can drink from the fount itself.

---

17 The action of Counter-Tradition is pure illusion, because precisely at that moment its triumph seems most complete, it will be destroyed by the action of those spiritual influences which will intervene to prepare the final 'straightening'. To light is opposed shadow, to Truth, lies. It is the part of every militant to hold fast and firm to his positions, lucid and conscious that Tradition is the unique means for reaffirming the Sacred in our world, mutilated as it is by malice and mendacity.

10.4 MILITANCY AND RELIGIOSITY

In day to day affairs, the militant of the Tradition comes face-to-face with a world which is ever more atheistic and materialistic, to which he opposes a sacred vision of life, a consideration of the divine which represents the centre around which his entire existence blooms and unfolds itself. For this reason, a secular, materialistic, agnostic or atheist militant is inconceivable.

For which reason, the first moment of clarity toward oneself requires an examination of one's true interior disposition: is one on the quest for God and the Sacred, does one wish to belong to a vision of the spiritual world and hierarchy? Or has one aligned oneself with the opposite view? A simple affirmative response will not suffice here, but one must rather be capable, once the choice has been made, to fight for the Tradition, to nourish one's interior tension, to be ready to renounce certain things in order to accept the duty of living and bearing witness to the Traditional Principles. To accept the front of Truth and Justice requires indeed an effort toward impeccability, beginning already from a comportment which does not allow blaspheming, inebriation, the use of drugs, being violent or vulgar. To make of the Sacred one's existential axis and to maintain Honour, Fidelity, Sacrifice, Gift, Loyalty — the Values for which one wishes to be the bearer — imposes on one above all a work of ascesis as a means of knowing and rectifying oneself, giving oneself a form and a discipline. Having clarified the premises, the rest will follow as consequence, and each will walk the path that most befits him, finding the proper balance between militancy and the practice of a religious confession.

This last, supposing only it is lived consciously and actively, will never stand in contrast to the Tradition, nor still less with militancy, but rather can become a staff along the path of rediscovering oneself and of knowledge. The important thing is to not limit one's quest to a simple superstitious form or to a devotional affair, in which one recalls God during moments of need, when one is afraid or feels defenceless, or when one hopes that one's desires will be realised. And at the same time, it is important not to fall into a fanatical confessionalism according to which there is no salvation outside of one's own parish.

For the man of Tradition, upright and impersonal action represents the first form of prayer necessary to bring out the luminous part of oneself, since, as Evola underlines, 'The "traditional man" should present himself as being as free from restraints and exterior forms, as he is solidly rooted in the common, invariable, perennial foundation of every great historical tradition. ... Ghibellinism, in its deepest aspect, believed more or less that through the concept of earthly life as discipline, militancy and service, the individual might be led beyond himself to pursue the supernatural end of the human personality, by way of action and under the insignia of the Imperium'.[18] For this reason, for the militant, 'reference to a reality and a transcendent order will suffice, reference to something which lies beyond what is usually human and what holds as simple individual earthly existence. This reference must not permit pietistic evasions or humanitarian excuses. It will serve for the grafting of a force other than human force, so as to attract an invisible consecration for a new world articulated by men and lords of men.'

The rooting of Traditional Values is already a sufficient condition for an interior bearing, the basis for a work of reconstruction through which one cannot pass by means of a comfortable choice, supposing oneself free from ethical precepts so as to embrace a 'do-it-yourself' religiosity. The principles, if they are to be deeply rooted and assimilated, must not be preached, but lived, that the individual's connection to a transcendent order might be something which goes effectively beyond morality and the fideistic attitude.

18   J. Evola, *Men Among the Ruins*, Chapter 10, 'Tradition — Catholicism — Ghibell inism'.

CONCLUSIONS

STYLE MAKES ACTION

TO BE ABLE TO become truly free, and to unchain oneself from the various bonds that impede one from taking flight, one must find in oneself that strength which presses one to act in an impersonal and disinterested way, observing each day one's own heart. One must act in daily reality so as to verify one's bearing, and only through an action void of any purely personal aim can we truly rectify the 'bastardised nature' of modern men. One must develop the capacity to open oneself without losing oneself, to give one's support without letting oneself be restrained thereby, considering existential experience in such a way as to know oneself and to develop one's personality. Thus, though one lives in an epoch of dissolution, one will not be deteriorated.

Toward this end, the militant must leverage upon his own will, which must not be *ut natura* (according to nature), which is to say purely instinctual or animal and fit for gestures aimed at satisfying physiological needs, but also and above all *ut libertas* (according to liberty), the single truly indispensable thing for whomever aspires to walk the path of rectification. This is the will necessary to conquer the numerous slaveries which bind one to the most uncontrolled need, slaveries of every kind: they regard personal interests, the appetites of the ego, of fears, of material things, of vices, etc. The heart is inevitably tied to a series of needs (desires) and fears, which are more or less alike and above all more or less false, and which impede a true comprehension of reality. To convenience, to luxury, to laziness, to egoism are twinned the fears of solitude or of being inadequate to confront certain situations, or the fear of being judged, of appearing in a certain way rather than in another, the anguish of renouncing little daily caresses and a typically bourgeois kind of safety — home, a warm bed, a good meal, etc. One cannot prescind from daily experimentation in the many occasions that life affords us, whether these are pleasant or not, difficult or apparently easy, expected or unexpected; one must use these to exorcise the mental conditionings that emerge within one continuously. Fears and desires are nothing other than products of the mind which, as usual, deform the nature of things.

To rectify the dark tendencies, therefore, means to awaken in oneself the Universal Principle, a result that one attains slowly, conquest after conquest, and for which great gestures are less needed than a continual standing one's ground and advancing. This is the style that must come to the fore, the style of the warrior who battles ceaselessly, careless of victory or defeat, because he knows that this is his destiny and he can do no other. Just as war is, from the Traditional point of view, the re-establishment of order, of peace and of unity, so the militant is the warrior dedicated to reconquering order, peace and unity above all within himself, so as to make himself a worthy witness to a renovated life, founded on Truth and Justice. All of this is the formation of the militant, a perfect marriage between knowledge, which is to say inspirational principle, and action, verification and confirmation. 'One must mind one thing alone: keeping oneself on one's feet in a world of ruins. If a generally efficacious action has, as has been said, the scarcest of possibilities, there remains to the troops, as has been suggested, internal defence. ... To render the values of truth, of reality, of the Tradition visible to those who, today, do not want "this" and who confusedly search for "something else", means to help see to it that the great temptation does not prevail in everyone, at that point where matter seems to have become stronger than the spirit.[1]

---

1   J. Evola, *Revolt Against the Modern World*, 'Conclusion'.

OTHER BOOKS PUBLISHED BY ARKTOS

OTHER BOOKS PUBLISHED BY ARKTOS

OTHER BOOKS PUBLISHED BY ARKTOS